ENGLISH PROSE

selected readings for liberal education

西方人文思想
选篇精读

苏耕欣 主编

复旦大学出版社

编写说明

　　编写这本教材的背景是当下中国大学积极与世界主流大学接轨这一基本趋势。接轨本身意味着存在差距，而在诸多差距中最为重要者莫过于理念。在过去很长一段时间里，我国大学的教育强调专业知识与技能，因此具有浓厚的职业培训色彩，而世界主流大学里本科教学虽然也教授专业知识、培养专业技能，但其最为核心的任务是素质教育，尤其是人格之塑造。素质教育的职责自然主要由人文学科各专业承担，因此，就大学本科教育而言，与世界接轨对于人文学科造成的影响最为深刻，而这其中外语专业更需要经历几乎是脱胎换骨式的改变。文史哲和理工农医等传统的专业在百年前业已形成完整的学科体系，人们对其如何发展了然于胸，并无异议，而外语专业则不然。在多数大学里，英语专业该教什么内容、做什么学问，仍是一个悬而未决的问题。在大量师资与教学工作仍然停留于语言教学的情况下，外语专业的接轨之路可谓道阻且长。

　　鉴于基础阅读课程在原有课程设置中的核心地位，对于这门课程的改革是我们摆脱这一困局的起点与关键步骤，而一些高校目前正在推行的通识教育也为外语专业之对外接轨提供了难得的契机。在西方一流大学里，外语专业的课程一般分成两部分：一是语言培训课程，数量不多，基本不涉思想内容，时常由对象国母语教师承担；二是文化课程，这些课程并不负责语言教学，大多用本国语言讲授，不少是全校通识教育板块中的重要组成部分。与这些国家的情况相比，我国英语专业的学生起点较高,完全可在本科阶段接受英语文化思想内容的课程。实际上,在国内一流大学里,就学生语言能力和文化素质而言,英语专业已经基本具备条件开设与英美大学水平大致相当的课程。

大学里的英语专业并非中学英语的延伸,也不是公共英语的"全日制版",这一基本认识是英语专业能够与世界主流大学成功接轨之关键。外语不是工具,外语专业的学生也不是语言机器;人文专业的学生理应善于思考,对于人自身和社会具备深刻的洞察力,视野宽阔的外语生尤其如此。人类诸多文化遗产都要通过英语来传承,因此英语专业在通识教育中占据重要地位,其学生通过四年的学习应该也能够在获得远高于非专业学生语言能力的同时,掌握西方文化的基本思想和发展脉络,对于英美乃至西方文化中的重要人物、著作和思想拥有较为深刻的理解与认识。这也是我们编写这本教材的指导思想。针对这一目标,我们选取了讨论西方尤其是英美文化各主要时期的论著,其中不少出自重要思想家、作家或学者之手,不仅思想深奥、语言精练、脍炙人口,还以思辨性见长,鼓励学生对于所涉问题进行批评性思考。过去的实践表明,这样的教材和课程有助于提高学生的思想素质和实用能力,也能够为培养部分优秀学生的学术兴趣创造良好的环境与条件。

针对教材中出现的重要人物、思想、流派和概念,我们以脚注、补充内容以及延伸阅读的形式提供了额外的资料。教师与学生还可利用工具书和网络等其他资源获取与课文内容相关的信息与资料。同时,我们还希望通过课后所配的问题和作文题目,鼓励学生结合自身生活经历,对于课文所涉社会与历史等议题进行评论与思考。

我们期待这本教材以及相应的课程为学生选修其他课程,学习其他更专、更深的内容做好语言和思想认识上的双重铺垫。

北京大学英语系的毛亮老师和复旦大学英语系的寿晨霖老师参与了本教材篇目的选择、编辑和整理工作。本教材在编写过程中还因复旦大学英语系部分师生的反馈与建议而获益匪浅。编者在此向以上师生一并致谢。

编者
2023 年 6 月于上海

Preface

We compiled this textbook with the awareness that in an increasingly specialized and fast-paced society, it is tempting to prioritize "useful" skills and dismiss knowledge in the arts and literature as mere adornments. Indeed, as technology seems to work wonders, the value of the humanities is in constant danger of being overlooked, questioned or even subject to ridicule. However, the condition of this age has made it equally clear to us that many challenges we face today have their origin in the wrong values we cherish and the misguided notions we possess, problems to which science and technology provide no effective solution. The best way to prepare the young generation for these challenges is an education in the humanities.

Studies in the humanities can achieve this goal because they help us become better human beings and make wiser choices. Unlike science and technology, works in literature, philosophy, history and art are themselves expressions of thought — ideas about and reflection upon our existence, purpose, and values. Through thought-provoking discussions on and encounters with great minds of the past and present, students can gain insights into the social, political, and cultural forces that have shaped our society, and acquire the necessary tools to navigate the complexities of the world beyond the college wall. Many of us have already realized that an education in the humanities accomplishes more than the mere transmission of knowledge; by enabling us to reach greater intellectual and moral heights, it acts as a force of progress. Working with great texts in these fields is a means of nurturing creativity, stimulating imagination, and cultivating a sense of cultural awareness. The benefits of such an education, as John Henry Newman would agree, do not end with its immediate results, but will translate in due course to an increased capacity to appreciate and connect with diverse perspectives, and to a heightened sense of responsibility, justice and open-mindedness. Attaining these objectives, meanwhile, does not preclude the humanities from being useful at the practical level. Great writings that have stood the test of time are the best training material for the acquisition of certain essential skills, for by dealing with complex ideas expressed in refined languages on a regular basis, students will develop the ability to see clearly, to think critically, and to communicate effectively.

Through the pages of this book, we embark on an intellectual voyage in Western thought from antiquity to the modern time by following the footsteps of its cultural heirs. Included in this anthology are excerpts of books and articles written by celebrated scholars, acclaimed writers or inspiring public figures, whose diction and style are well suited to the task of improving reading and writing skills. Students are also encouraged to extract from these texts ideas and voices that they can relate to, and principles and ideals that they may put faith in. Indeed, I flatter myself by hoping that this collection, for all its imperfections and omissions, will outlive its immediate purpose by serving as the prelude to a lifelong journey of joy-filled intellectual exploration.

Contents

The Idea of a University / 001

The Way of the Greeks / 009

The Decline and Fall of the Roman Empire / 018

The Decline and Fall of Literature / 026

Courtly Love / 042

What Is Humanism? / 053

Salt / 063

Progress / 069

Of Sympathy / 084

Civilization and Culture / 097

Federalist Papers, No. 10 / 105

A Vindication of the Rights of Woman / 112

The Imitation of Our Lord Don Quixote / 121

Of Individuality / 130

The Natural History of German Life / 142

The Soul of Man under Socialism / 164

Letter from a Birmingham Jail / 175

The Idea of a University[1]

... Philosophy, or Science, is related to Knowledge in this way: Knowledge is called by the name of Science or Philosophy, when it is acted upon, informed, or if I may use a strong figure, impregnated by Reason. Reason is the principle of that intrinsic fecundity of Knowledge, which, to those who possess it, is its especial value, and which dispenses with the necessity of their looking abroad for any end to rest upon external to itself. Knowledge, indeed, when thus exalted into a scientific form, is also power; not only is it excellent in itself, but whatever such excellence may be, it is something more, it has a result beyond itself. Doubtless; but that is a further consideration, with which I am not concerned. I only say that, prior to its being a power, it is a good; that it is, not only an instrument, but an end. I know well it may resolve itself into an art, and terminate in a mechanical process, and in tangible fruit; but it also may fall back upon that Reason which informs it, and resolve itself into Philosophy. In one case it is called Useful Knowledge, in the other Liberal. The same person may cultivate it

---

[1] Excerpted from "Discourse 5 Knowledge Its Own End" of John Henry Newman's lectures delivered in Dublin at the newly founded Catholic University of Ireland, published in 1852 and later titled *The Idea of a University*.

in both ways at once; but this again is a matter foreign to my subject; here I do but say that there are two ways of using Knowledge, and in matter of fact those who use it in one way are not likely to use it in the other, or at least in a very limited measure.

You see, then, here are two methods of Education; the end of the one is to be philosophical, of the other to be mechanical; the one rises towards general ideas, the other is exhausted upon what is particular and external. Let me not be thought to deny the necessity, or to decry the benefit, of such attention to what is particular and practical, as belongs to the useful or mechanical arts; life could not go on without them; we owe our daily welfare to them; their exercise is the duty of the many, and we owe to the many a debt of gratitude for fulfilling that duty. I only say that Knowledge, in proportion as it tends more and more to be particular, ceases to be Knowledge ... When I speak of Knowledge, I mean something intellectual, something which grasps what it perceives through the senses; something which takes a view of things; which sees more than the senses convey; which reasons upon what it sees, and while it sees; which invests it with an idea. It expresses itself, not in a mere enunciation, but by an enthymeme:[1] it is of the nature of science from the first, and in this consists its dignity. The principle of real dignity in Knowledge, its worth, its desirableness, considered irrespectively of its results, is this germ within it of a scientific or a philosophical process. This is how it comes to be an end in itself; this is why it admits of being called Liberal. Not to know the relative disposition of things is the state of slaves or children; to have mapped out the Universe is the boast, or at least the ambition, of Philosophy.

Moreover, such knowledge is not a mere extrinsic or accidental advantage, which is ours today and another's tomorrow, which may be got up from a book, and easily forgotten again, which we can command or

---

1 A syllogism in which one of the premises is understood but not present.

communicate at our pleasure, which we can borrow for the occasion, carry about in our hand and take into the market; it is an acquired illumination, it is a habit, a personal possession, and an inward endowment. And this is the reason why it is more correct, as well as more usual, to speak of a University as a place of education than of instruction, though, when knowledge is concerned, instruction would at first sight have seemed the more appropriate word. We are instructed, for instance, in manual exercises, in the fine and useful arts, in trades, and in ways of business; for these are methods, which have little or no effect upon the mind itself, are contained in rules committed to memory, to tradition, or to use, and bear upon an end external to themselves. But education is a higher word; it implies an action upon our mental nature, and the formation of a character; it is something individual and permanent, and is commonly spoken of in connection with religion and virtue. When, then, we speak of the communication of Knowledge as being Education, we thereby really imply that that Knowledge is a state or condition of mind; and since cultivation of mind is surely worth seeking for its own sake, we are thus brought once more to the conclusion, which the word "Liberal" and the word "Philosophy" have already suggested, that there is a Knowledge, which is desirable, though nothing come of it, as being of itself a treasure, and a sufficient remuneration of years of labor.

10.

... Today I have confined myself to saying that that training of the intellect, which is best for the individual himself, best enables him to discharge his duties to society. The Philosopher, indeed, and the man of the world differ in their very notion, but the methods, by which they are respectively formed, are pretty much the same. The Philosopher has the same command of matters of thought, which the true citizen and gentleman has of matters of business and conduct. If then a practical end must be assigned to a University course, I say it is that of training good members of society. Its art is the art of social life, and its end is fitness for the world. It neither confines its views to particular professions on the one hand, nor creates heroes or inspires genius on the other. Works indeed of genius fall under no art; heroic minds come under no rule; a University is not a birthplace of poets or of immortal authors, of founders of schools, leaders of colonies, or conquerors of nations. It does not promise a generation of Aristotles or Newtons, of Napoleons or Washingtons, or Raphaels or Shakespeares, though such miracles of nature it has before now contained within its precincts. Nor is it content on the other hand with forming the critic or the experimentalist, the economist or the engineer, though such too it includes within its scope. But a University training is the great ordinary means to a great but ordinary end; it aims at raising the intellectual tone of society, at cultivating the public mind, at purifying the national taste, at supplying true principles to popular enthusiasm and fixed aims to popular aspiration, at giving enlargement and sobriety to the ideas of the age, at facilitating the exercise of political power, and refining the intercourse of private life. It is the education which gives a man a clear conscious view of his own opinions and judgments, a truth in developing them, an eloquence in expressing them, and a force in urging them. It teaches him to see things as they are, to go right to the point, to disentangle a skein of thought, to detect what is sophistical, and to discard what is irrelevant. It prepares him to fill any post with credit, and to master any subject with facility. It shows him how to accommodate himself to others, how to throw himself into their state of mind, how to bring before them his own, how to influence them, how to come to an understanding with them, how to bear with them. He is at home in any society, he has common ground with every class; he knows when to speak and when to be silent; he is able to converse, he is able to listen; he can ask a question pertinently, and gain a lesson seasonably, when he has nothing to impart himself; he is ever ready, yet never in the way; he is a pleasant companion, and a comrade you can depend upon; he knows when to be serious and when to trifle, and he has a sure tact which enables him to trifle with gracefulness and to be serious with effect. He has the repose of a mind which lives in itself, while it lives in the world, and which has resources for its happiness at home when it cannot go abroad. He has a gift which serves him in public, and supports him in retirement, without which good fortune is but vulgar, and with which failure and disappointment have a charm. The art which tends to make a man all this is in the object which it pursues as useful as the art of wealth or the art of health, though it is less susceptible of method, and less tangible, less certain, less complete in its result.

I. Supplementary information

1. John Henry Newman

John Henry Newman (1801–1890) was an influential theologian, philosopher, and educator in the 19th century, and was probably best known for his role in the Oxford Movement, which sought to bring the Church of England back to its Catholic roots.

Newman's intellectual journey went through several phases, starting as an evangelical Anglican and eventually leading him to convert to Roman Catholicism in 1845. This conversion was a significant event that shaped the rest of his life and had a profound impact on his writings and teachings.

Throughout his career, Newman authored several influential works, including *The Idea of a University* and *Apologia Pro Vita Sua*, among others. These writings explore themes such as education, the relationship between faith and reason, the nature of religious belief, and the importance of tradition.

Newman's approach to education pays special attention to the holistic development of individuals, combining intellectual pursuits with moral and spiritual formation. He believes in the importance of liberal arts education, where students would engage with a wide range of disciplines to cultivate skills in critical thinking and acquire a broader understanding of the world. Newman has produced profound influence on the development of the modern university in the West.

2. Rise of the University and the English College System

The modern university owes it origin mainly to the training of ecclesiastics in the Middle Ages. The first university in the modern sense was founded in Bologna, Italy, in 1088. In its early stage, the school was largely an association or a guild of teachers and scholars for teaching particular crafts (law in the case of Bologna). Oxford and Cambridge, the oldest universities in England, were founded in the 12th and 13th centuries and remained the only universities in England until 1828, when University of London was established.

In medieval Bologna the body of instructors was known as the *collegium* and the student body the *universitas*. In most universities of the later Middle Ages, *collegium* meant an endowed residence hall for students, usually candidates for both bachelor and advanced degrees. The colleges had their own libraries and scientific instruments and offered regular salaries to doctors and tutors who could prepare students to be examined for degrees. That a college trains for a degree and a university grants it was the dominant 19th-century British idea of higher education.

In Ireland university colleges were founded by Roman Catholics in the 1850s. Newman delivered his first valuable literary work *The Scope and Nature of University Education*, a collection of lectures, to the University of Dublin, of which he became Rector in 1854.

In the United States, the school that adopts an English-style college system is Yale University, where each of the fourteen residential colleges supposedly represents Yale in microcosm, offering students a sense of intimate social and intellectual connection, as well as a space of civic and moral responsibility.

II. Questions to think about as you read the text

1. If both types of knowledge are necessary for Newman, what is the point of making the distinction?
2. What new understanding of the word "liberal" have you acquired through the reading of Newman's lectures?

III. Suggested essay topics

1. Write an essay evaluating your brief experience of university by the standard of John Henry Newman.
2. My idea of a university.

IV. Further reading

1. Booth, Wayne C., ed. *The Knowledge Most Worth Having*. Chicago University Press, 1967.

2. The Interesting Origin of the University of Oxford

The founding of Oxford was a by-product of the conflict between the Crown and the Church in England in the Middle Ages. In 1155 Thomas Becket was appointed by King Henry II as his Chancellor. Becket soon became the King's confidant, and was made the Archbishop of Canterbury, the chief bishop and principal leader of the Church of England, when Theobald, his predecessor, died in 1161. Henry, needless to say, expected Becket to be supportive of him on important issues of the state, but their friendship was put to the test when it became clear that Becket took his responsibilities as Archbishop very seriously and would defend the Church against the Crown. One matter in particular, the "Benefit of Clergy", highlighted this rift. The clergy enjoyed many privileges in the Middle Ages, one of which was certain special legal treatment. When clerics were charged with crimes, for example, the church reserved the right to try them in the ecclesiastical courts instead of those of the Crown. Henry was determined to put an end to this practice, but Becket, to his disappointment, resisted the king's attempt. In 1164, sensing that he was in serious danger as a result of this conflict, Becket fled into exile in France. He came back to renew the struggle six years later.

An unintended but important result of this tug-of-war between the Crown and the Church over ecclesiastical privileges was the establishment of the University of Oxford. To deprive the archbishop of the support he enjoyed while abroad, Henry ordered home all the English students who had gathered at Paris (many being trained there for the church). Almost immediately, they started a university of their own (1167), from which, in 1209, a rebellious group split off to form the University of Cambridge.

In 1170 Becket returned to England, only to be murdered by the King's men at the Canterbury Cathedral, apparently a consequence of the failure to resolve his conflict with the king. The Christian world was outraged at the murder. Pope Alexander III canonized Becket (i.e., made him a "saint") in 1173. A shrine was set up in Canterbury, which quickly became a place of pilgrimage. The pilgrims in Chaucer's masterpiece *The Canterbury Tales* travel to Canterbury precisely for the purpose of paying tribute to Saint Thomas.

The Way of the Greeks[1]

Character is a Greek word, but it did not mean to the Greeks what it means to us. To them it stood first for the mark stamped upon the coin, and then for the impress of this or that quality upon a man, as Euripides[2] speaks of the stamp — character — of valor upon Hercules, man the coin, valor the mark imprinted on him. To us a man's character is that which is peculiarly his own; it distinguishes each one from the rest. To the Greeks it was a man's share in qualities all men partake of; it united each one to the rest. We are interested in people's special characteristics, the things in this or that person which are different from the general. The Greeks, on the contrary, thought what was important in a man were precisely the qualities he shared with all mankind.

The distinction is a vital one. Our way is to consider each separate thing alone by itself; the Greeks always saw things as parts of a whole, and this habit of mind is stamped upon everything they did. It is the underlying cause of the difference between their art and ours. Architecture, perhaps, is the

---

1 Excerpted from Edith Hamilton, *The Greek Way* (New York and London: Norton, 1993), pp.229–31, 250 and 252.
2 Euripides (c. 484–406 BCE), Greek tragic dramatist, author of such plays as *Medea* (431 BCE), *Hippolytus* (428 BCE), *Andromache* (426? BCE) and *Hecuba* (425? BCE).

clearest illustration. The greatest buildings since Greek days, the cathedrals of the Middle Ages, were built, it would seem, without any regard to their situation, placed haphazard, wherever it was convenient. Almost invariably a cathedral stands low down in the midst of a huddle of little houses, often as old or older, where it is marked by its incongruity with the surroundings. The situation of the building did not enter into[1] the architects' plans. They were concerned only with the cathedral itself. The idea never occurred to them to think of it in relation to what was around it. It was not part of a whole to them; it was the whole. But to the Greek architect the setting of his temple was all-important. He planned it, seeing it in clear outline against sea or sky, determining its size by its situation on plain hilltop or the wide plateau of an acropolis. It dominated the scene, indeed; it became through his genius the most important feature in it, but it was always a part of it. He did not think of it in and for itself, as just the building he was making; he conceived of it in relation to the hills and the seas and the arch of the sky.

To see anything in relation to other things is to see it simplified. A house is a very complicated matter considered by itself: plan, decoration, furnishings; each room, indeed, made up of many things; but, if it is considered as part of a block or part of a city, the details sink out of sight. Just as a city in itself is a mass of complexity but is reduced to a few essentials when it is thought of as belonging to a country. The earth shows an infinite diversity, but in relation to the universe it is a sphere swinging in space, nothing more.

So the Greek temple, conceived of as a part of its setting, was simplified, the simplest of all the great buildings of the world, and the Gothic cathedral, seen as a complete whole in itself, unrelated to anything beyond itself, was of all buildings the most elaborated in detail.

---

1 *enter into*: [usually in negatives] to affect a situation and be something that you consider when you make a choice (Longman).

This necessity of the Greek mind to see everything in relation to a whole made the Greek drama what it is just as it made the Greek temple. The characters in a Greek play are not like the characters in any other drama. The Greek tragedians' way of drawing a human being belongs to them alone of all playwrights. They saw people simplified, because, just as in the case of their temples, they saw them as part of a whole. As they looked at human life, the protagonist was not human; the chief role was played by that which underlies the riddle of the world, that Necessity which brings us here and takes us hence, which gives good to one and evil to another, which visits the sins of the fathers upon the children and sweeps away innocent and guilty in fire and pestilence and earthquake shock. "Shall the thing formed say to him that formed it, Why hast thou made me thus? Hath not the potter power over the clay to make one vessel unto honor and another unto dishonor?" To St. Paul[1] the puzzle was easy to solve. To the Greek tragedians it was the enigma never to be answered and they thought of human beings first and foremost in relation to that mystery. So placed against "the background of infinity," part of an immeasurable whole, human complexities are simplified. The accidental and the trivial, from the point of view of the whole, drop out of sight, as in a wide landscape figures can be seen only in outline, or as the innumerable lines on one of Rembrandt's old women's faces would disappear if she were placed in a spacious setting.

For us it is the other way about. Each human being fills an entire canvas. We have dismissed from our scheme of things fate that spins the thread and cuts it. Human nature is the great enigma to us; the mystery of life is the mystery of a man's own self and the conflict we care about goes on within. A

---

1 Saint Paul (?3–?68): a Christian apostle whose original name was Saul of Tarsus. After becoming a Christian, he changed his name to Paul and spent the rest of his life teaching people about Jesus, whom, incidentally, he never met in person. He wrote many of the epistles in the New Testament of the Bible and his work facilitated the spread of Christianity in the Roman Empire.

man's life is seen not as what is done to him but as what he does to himself, the fault not in our stars but in ourselves, and there is a stage where each one of us is the only actor. We differ from the Greeks in nothing so much as in the way we look at the individual, isolated, in and for himself. Our drama, all our art, is the very reverse of simplified. It is a work of most subtle individualization.

But to the Greek, human beings were not chiefly different but chiefly alike. The Greek dramatists, placing their characters on the tremendous stage whose drama is the conflict between man and the power that shapes him, man "created sick, commanded to be whole," saw as important in them only the dominant traits, the great emotions, the terrors and desires and sorrows and hatreds, that belong to all mankind and to all generations and make the unchanging pattern of human life. Put any character from a Greek tragedy beside one of Shakespeare's and the difference that results from the different points of view is clearly to be seen. One is simple and uncomplicated; the other complex and contradictory too.

...

A Greek temple makes the spectator aware of the wideness and the wonder of sea and sky and mountain range as he could not be if that shining marvel of white stone were not there in sharp relief against them, and, in the same way, a Greek tragedy brings before us the strangeness that surrounds us, the dark unknown our life is bounded by, through the suffering of a great soul given to us so simply and so powerfully, we know in it all human anguish and the mystery of pain.

But simplicity of characterization is not the same thing as lack of characterization. It is true in fact that characters simply drawn are almost never distinctly individualized, but Greek tragedy is the great example of how it can be done. The personages of a Greek play are clearly characterized.

...

Life is what the spirit is concerned with, the individual. Abstractions from life are what the mind is concerned with, the classified, the type. The Greeks were concerned with both. They wanted to know what things are and what things mean. They did not lose the individual in the type nor the type in the individual, Tartuffe's universal truth or Falstaff's living reality.[1] The most familiar of all the sayings that has come down to us from classic times was spoken indeed by a Roman but it is a purely Greek conception, the basic idea of one of the greatest of Greek philosophies, "I am a man and nothing in mankind do I hold alien to me."

...

It is an achievement possible only when mind and spirit are balanced. The mind simplifies, for it sees everything related, everything part of a whole, as Christ in the Gospel story is the mediator between God and man. The spirit individualizes. The figure of the Son of Man, so depicted that throughout the centuries a great multitude which no man could number, of all nations and kindreds and peoples and tongues, have suffered with Him and understood through Him, is the creation of the spirit.

So too the characters in Greek drama were the result of the Greek balance, individuals that showed a truth for all humanity in every human being, mankind in a man. The Greek mind that must see a thing never in and for itself but always connected with what was greater, and the Greek spirit that saw beauty and meaning in each separate thing, made Greek tragedy as they made Greek sculpture and Greek architecture, each an example of something completely individual at once simplified and given its significance by being always seen as connected with something universal, an expression

---

1   Tartuffe, eponymous character in *Tartuffe*, also called *The Impostor* or *The Hypocrite*, a play written by the French author Molière in 1664. It is one of Molière's most famous theatrical comedies. Falstaff, a character in the plays *Henry IV* (Parts 1 and 2) and *The Merry Wives of Windsor* by William Shakespeare. Falstaff is a friend of the prince and later King Henry V. A fat friendly old man, he enjoys having fun, drinks too much alcohol, and is not always completely honest.

of the Greek ideal, "beauty, absolute, simple, and everlasting ... the irradiation of the particular by the general."

I. Supplementary information

The Importance of Ancient Greece to Western Civilization

Ancient Greece is one of the two most important sources of influence on Western civilization, the other being Christianity. The imprint of the ancient Greeks on Western society can be seen in such diverse areas as politics, philosophy, science, art, architecture and sports.

In politics, the ancient Greek experimentation with democracy is of exceptional importance to the West. The democratic ideals and the institutionalization of assemblies elected by the people, which were first incubated in Athens, still serve as the foundation of the Western forms of government.

Western philosophy and science owe an equally huge debt to the Greeks. Scientists such as Pythagoras and Euclid made important advances in mathematics and astronomy. In the field of philosophy, almost all of Western thought traces its origins back to the core Greek thinkers, particularly Socrates, Plato and Aristotle.

The influence of ancient Greece in the fields of art and architecture is much more "visible." Greek attention to the beauty of the human form, thanks in part to the revival of interest in classical antiquity during the Renaissance and Neo-Classical period, has profoundly "shaped" Western portraiture and sculpting. The Greek style of architecture, along with the ideas and values that it embodies, also saw its rebirth in the 18th century. The style of both the

White House and the US Capitol Building, for example, is Greek in origin.

The impact of Greek literature cannot possibly be overestimated, either. Greek writers such as Homer, Hesiod, Sappho, Aeschylus and Sophocles, have contributed inestimably to Western literature, in the forms of core stories, literary motifs and mythic references.

It continues to intrigue scholars why Greece, a country so small in size and wealth, is so huge in influence.

II. Questions to think about as you read the text

1. How does a Greek temple reflect the ideas of the Greeks?
2. Find images of Gothic cathedrals and Greek temples. Discuss their difference.
3. Why is the individual associated with spirit while the type with the mind, according to the author?

III. Suggested essay topics

1. Write an essay explaining how a certain aspect or object of Western culture, with which you are familiar, owes its origin to ancient Greece.
2. Based on your perhaps still limited knowledge about ancient Greece, write an essay discussing what you perceive to be the affinity or the lack thereof between Greek and Chinese cultures.

IV. Further reading

The Greco-Buddhist Civilization

The Greco-Buddhist civilization in Central Asia was a unique and fascinating cultural and artistic fusion that emerged during the period from the 2nd century BCE to the 5th century CE. It developed as a result of the interaction between Greek and Buddhist cultures in the regions of Bactria (modern-day Afghanistan) and Gandhara (parts of present-day Pakistan and Afghanistan). This civilization represents more than a mere exchange of ideas, aesthetics, and artistic styles between Hellenistic and Buddhist traditions; it was a deep intertwining of their cultural elements.

The Greek presence in the region brought Hellenistic influences, including art, philosophy, and administrative systems. Buddhism, which had spread from India, blended with local traditions. The result was a syncretic civilization with a distinct artistic and intellectual character.

One of the remarkable legacies of this Greco-Buddhist civilization is its artistic output. The region witnessed the creation of exquisite sculptures, frescoes, and other artworks that combined Greek and Buddhist artistic traditions. Influenced by the Hellenistic style, the sculptures often depicted Buddha and bodhisattvas with a blend of Greek and Indian features. The Gandhara school of art, in particular, produced iconic representations of Buddha and Buddhist narratives, showcasing a harmonious amalgamation of Greek naturalism and Buddhist spiritual symbolism. The influence of Greek naturalism can be observed in the realistic rendering of facial features, hairstyles, and drapery, while the spiritual symbolism of Buddhism is conveyed through the serene expressions and hand gestures (mudras) associated with Buddhist iconography. In fact, historians argue that the very image of Buddha, which did not appear in India until at least five hundred years after his death, was inspired by images in Greek mythology.

The Bactrian kingdom, centered around the region of Bactria (modern-day Afghanistan), also witnessed the impact of Greek artistic styles. Bactrian bronze statues, dating from the 2nd century BCE to the 3rd century CE, display a synthesis of Greek and Buddhist influences. These statues often depict standing or seated figures of Buddhist deities or bodhisattvas adorned with Hellenistic-inspired garments and accessories, such as flowing robes, belts, and diadems. The treatment of the human form in these statues reflects the influence of Greek idealism and anatomical proportions.

Greek influence is also reflected in the architecture of these Central Asian kingdoms. Friezes and relief panels found in Buddhist monastic complexes and stupas in this region, for example, demonstrate the intermingling of Greek and Buddhist artistic traditions. These decorative elements often depict scenes from the life of Buddha, Jataka tales (stories of Buddha's previous lives), or divine figures. The friezes incorporate Greek-inspired architectural motifs, such as Ionic or Corinthian columns, into the Buddhist context. The rendering of figures and drapery in these reliefs combines Hellenistic naturalism with Buddhist iconographic conventions, creating a distinctive artistic style.

Greco-Buddhist fusion was not limited to works of art, but involved more practical aspects of life. Coins minted by these kingdoms, among others, often feature Greek-inspired motifs, such as Greek gods, portraits of Hellenistic rulers, and Greek inscriptions alongside Buddhist symbols and Indian deities. These objects, which abound in Central Asia, bear witness to the power of the naturalistic aesthetics of Greek art, the form which gave expression to the spiritual symbolism of Buddhism.

The Decline and Fall of the Roman Empire

A.H.M. Jones, a prominent historian of the 20th century, offered a nuanced perspective on the decline and fall of the Roman Empire. He argued that the decline was a complex process involving a combination of internal and external factors. While he acknowledged the impact of external threats, such as barbarian invasions and economic pressures, Jones went to great lengths to discuss the significance of internal weaknesses. According to Jones, the erosion of traditional Roman values, administrative inefficiency, social unrest, and the declining civic spirit among the ruling elite played crucial roles in the empire's decline. He viewed the decline as a gradual and multifaceted process rather than a sudden collapse, highlighting the interconnectedness of political, social, and cultural factors in shaping the fate of the Roman Empire. Following is an excerpt of his article, which focuses on the roles of civic spirit and religion in the decline of Rome.

It is hardly possible to assign reasons for the mysterious changes

---

[1] Excerpted from A. H. M. Jones, "The Decline and Fall of the Roman Empire," *History*, Oct, 1955, New Series, Vol. 40, No. 140 (Oct, 1955), pp. 209–26.

which come over man's whole attitude to life from one age to another. The historian can do little more than register them. In the classical age of Greek and Roman civilization, when the city was the effective political unit, it was the city that dominated men's thoughts and emotions. Religion was in the main a communal activity, the worship by the citizens of the gods who protected their city. The virtues which were valued were the civic virtues, courage in fighting for one's city, wisdom and public spirit in guiding its policy, and open-handed generosity in contributing to its expenses. The average man seems to have found satisfaction in the service of his city: he had no hankering for personal immortality, being content to live on in the memory of his fellow citizens, and felt no need for personal communion with the divine powers. The political subjection of cities to kings and ultimately to Rome inevitably weakened civic spirit. Many of its outlets were cut off. As Plutarch[1] regretfully remarks, under the all-embracing rule of Rome a man could no longer win glory by leading his fellow citizens to victory in war, nor by statesmanlike handling of a political crisis. Civic patriotism survived the political extinction of the city for a surprisingly long period, but, deprived of useful outlets, it was diverted into futile backwaters and ultimately sank into stagnation. Now that cities could no longer fight one another for freedom or empire they carried on bitter feuds over questions of precedence and honorific titles, and vied with one another in competitive building programmes and games and festivals. Now that any challenge to the oligarchies which the Roman government supported was ruthlessly suppressed as sedition, internal politics degenerated into personal rivalries, in which, as Plutarch is forced to admit, ability or merit counted for little and the issue was decided by the wealth of the candidates and their willingness to spend it lavishly for the city's glory. This competition

---

1 Plutarch (?46–?120), an ancient Greek historian whose main work was *Plutarch's Lives*, which is a biography about famous Greek and Roman politicians and military leaders.

in extravagance between cities and between individuals was no doubt less destructive than the internecine wars and the party struggles which had been the bane of the sovereign city state. But it was economically ruinous, and led to an increasingly strict surveyance by the imperial government of local administration, especially on its financial side, with a corresponding decay of civic initiative, and to a growing distaste for local politics on the part of the wealthy, who alone could take any active part in them. Local politics were not only losing their savour, now that the cities were mere cogs in the imperial administrative machine, but were becoming a positive nuisance, since they involved a heavy expenditure. Even the members of the governing oligarchies began to regard local office as a burdensome responsibility and to seek ways and means of evading it.

While civic spirit decayed, there was no growth of imperial patriotism. From the first the imperial government had been regarded as an external power, at worst an oppressive tyrant, whose agents extorted taxes and levied recruits and exploited the provincials on their own account, at best a benevolent protector, which maintained armies to defend the provinces against the barbarians, and assured internal peace and order. The ideal relation of the cities of the empire to the imperial government was aptly expressed by the official cult of Rome and Augustus, whereby the provincial communities manifested their humble gratitude to the benefits received and prayed for their continuance for all time. The ordinary citizen's role was purely passive, in most cases limited to paying his taxes. He neither felt, nor was encouraged to feel, any sense of responsibility for the welfare, or even for the survival, of the empire. His loyalty was passive, not active.

...

Concurrently with, and perhaps in compensation for, the decay of civic spirit there was a growth of personal religion. Its origin can be traced back to the Hellenistic age, in the rise of philosophic systems like Cynicism,

Stoicism and Epicureanism, which sought to establish a standard of values and inculcate a way of life for the individual, isolated from his community. On a more emotional level it is expressed in the growing popularity of mystery religions, in which the individual worshipper sought communion with the divine, and was encouraged in hopes of individual survival beyond the grave. These two streams ultimately coalesced in the mystical Neoplatonism[1] which dominated educated paganism from the third century onwards. According to this creed the world of sense was illusory or evil, and the soul found fulfilment by shaking itself free from its earthly shackles and rising into the world of ideas with the ultimate goal of communion with the Absolute.

Christianity likewise inculcated indifference to the things of this world. The earliest generations of Christians, living in eager expectation of the Second Coming of the Lord, were naturally uninterested in the world around them. And as this hope became less vivid, they concentrated on the life of the spirit and the world to come. There was a school of thought which regarded the empire as a satanic organization. Most Christians, however, were not positively hostile to the empire and indeed regarded it as of divine institution. But even when it became Christian it inspired no sense of loyalty or devotion. Christians did not feel called upon to fight for its survival or to remedy its abuses, because their eyes were fixed on the salvation of individual souls. The calamities of the empire were regarded not as challenges to action, but as tribulations sent by God to purify the righteous and call sinners to repentance.

This outlook on life not only bred a generally defeatist attitude to the problems of the time, which must have weakened the resistance of

---

[1] Platonism modified in later antiquity to accord with Aristotelian, post-Aristotelian, and eastern conceptions that conceive of the world as an emanation from an ultimate indivisible being with whom the soul is capable of being reunited in trance or ecstasy. It was later incorporated into Christian theology.

the empire, but produced specific movements which undoubtedly to some degree diminished its strength. Prominent among these is monasticism, the complete abandonment of this world for a life of spiritual contemplation. The movement reached vast proportions, especially in the East, and must have sterilized a significant proportion of the empire's failing manpower. For hermits and monks were, of course, lost as potential recruits to the army and the administration. The rare attempts of the imperial government to assert the claims of the public service were bitterly resisted by the church.

I. Supplementary information

The Rise of Christianity in the Roman Empire

The rise of Christianity in the Roman Empire was a significant event that changed the history of the Western, indeed, the whole, world. Initially considered a small and marginalized sect, Christianity gradually gained traction and grew in popularity within the diverse Roman society. Several factors contributed to its rise, including the appeal of its teachings, its emphasis on monotheism in a polytheistic culture, and its message of salvation and eternal life. The martyrdom of early Christian believers also played a crucial role in attracting attention and inspiring devotion among followers. Moreover, the patronage of influential figures, such as Emperor Constantine, who legalized Christianity through the Edict of Milan in 313 CE, provided a turning point for the religion's acceptance and subsequent spread throughout the empire. The rise of Christianity marked a significant transformation in the religious and cultural landscape of the Roman Empire, eventually leading to its establishment as the dominant faith within the realm.

The core teachings of traditional Christianity revolve around the belief that Jesus is the Son of God, the second person of the Trinity, and that his life, crucifixion, resurrection, and ascension into heaven demonstrate God's love and forgiveness for humanity. Salvation and eternal life are attainable through faith in Jesus, as stated in the Bible, specifically the New Testament, while Christians also recognize the Old Testament as sacred and authoritative scripture. Christian ethics have roots in the Jewish tradition, particularly the Ten Commandments, although interpretations may differ based on the teachings and practices of Jesus. Christianity is characterized by its corporate worship, sacraments, and the involvement of trained clergy in organized churches. However, there exists a wide range of worship styles, interpretations of clergy roles, and variations in church organization within the Christian faith.

II. Questions to think about as you read the text

1. The author has listed several specific factors that contributed to the decline and fall of the Roman Empire. Do these factors show any common tendency?
2. What conflicts seemed to characterize the Roman Empire as described in this excerpt?

III. Suggested essay topics

1. If Rome had not fallen ...
2. If you were a Roman ruler in the waning years of the empire, what would you do about Christianity that would possibly save Rome?

IV. Further reading

The Decline and Fall of the Roman Empire[1]

The passive and unresisting obedience, which bows under the yoke of authority, or even of oppression, must have appeared, in the eyes of an absolute monarch, the most conspicuous and useful of the evangelic virtues. The primitive Christians derived the institution of civil government, not from the consent of the people, but from the decrees of Heaven. The reigning emperor, though he had usurped the sceptre by treason and murder, immediately assumed the sacred character of vicegerent of the Deity. To the Deity alone he was accountable for the abuse of his power; and his subjects were indissolubly bound, by their oath of fidelity, to a tyrant, who had violated every law of nature and society. The humble Christians were sent into the world as sheep among wolves; and since they were not permitted to employ force even in the defence of their religion, they should be still more criminal if they were tempted to shed the blood of their fellow-creatures in disputing the vain privileges, or the sordid possessions, of this transitory life. Faithful to the doctrine of the apostle, who in the reign of Nero had preached the duty of unconditional submission, the Christians of the three first centuries preserved their conscience pure and innocent of the guilt of secret conspiracy, or open rebellion. While they experienced the rigor of persecution, they were never provoked either to meet their tyrants in the field, or indignantly to withdraw themselves into some remote and sequestered corner of the globe. The Protestants of France, of Germany, and of Britain, who asserted with such intrepid courage their civil and religious freedom, have been insulted by the invidious comparison between the conduct of the primitive and of the reformed Christians. Perhaps, instead of censure, some applause may be due to the superior sense and spirit of our

---

1　Edward Gibbon, *The Decline and Fall of the Roman Empire*, Vol. II (London: David Campbell Publishers, 1993), 255–56.

ancestors, who had convinced themselves that religion cannot abolish the unalienable rights of human nature. Perhaps the patience of the primitive church may be ascribed to its weakness, as well as to its virtue. A sect of unwarlike plebeians, without leaders, without arms, without fortifications, must have encountered inevitable destruction in a rash and fruitless resistance to the master of the Roman legions. But the Christians, when they deprecated the wrath of Diocletian, or solicited the favor of Constantine, could allege, with truth and confidence, that they held the principle of passive obedience, and that, in the space of three centuries, their conduct had always been conformable to their principles. They might add, that the throne of the emperors would be established on a fixed and permanent basis, if all their subjects, embracing the Christian doctrine, should learn to suffer and to obey.

The Decline and Fall of Literature[1]

An answer that leads back, I believe, to the core of a literary education is to be found in an entry Emerson[2] made in his journal 165 years ago. "The whole secret of the teacher's force," he wrote, "lies in the conviction that men are convertible. And they are. They want awakening." Having left the ministry two years before, Emerson was still in the process of transforming himself from a preacher into a lecturer, and of altering the form of his writing from the sermon to the essay. But his motive for speaking and writing had not changed with the shedding of his frock. Like every great teacher, he was in the business of trying to "get the soul out of bed, out of her deep habitual sleep."

None of us who has ever been a student can fail to read this passage without remembering some teacher by whom we were startled out of complacency about our own ignorance. For this to take place, the student must be open to it, and the teacher must overcome the incremental fatigue of repetitive work and somehow remain a *professor* in the religious sense of that

---

1   Excerpted from Andrew Delbanco, "The Decline and Fall of Literature," *The New York Review of Books*, November 4, 1999. Copyright © 1999, Andrew Delbanco. Reprinted with permission from original publisher.
2   Ralph Waldo Emerson (1803–1882), American lecturer, poet, and essayist, the leading exponent of New England Transcendentalism.

word — ardent, exemplary, even fanatic.

Literary studies, in fact, have their roots in religion. Trilling[1] understood this when he remarked, in his gloomy essay about the future of the humanities, that "the educated person" had traditionally been conceived as an initiate who began as a postulant, passed to a higher level of experience, and became worthy of admission into the company of those who are thought to have transcended the mental darkness and inertia in which they were previously immersed.

Such a view of education as illumination and deliverance following what Trilling called "exigent experience" is entirely Emersonian.[2] It has little to do with the positivist idea of education to which the modern research university is chiefly devoted — learning "how to extend, even by minute accretions, the realm of knowledge."[3] This corporate notion of knowledge as a growing sum of discoveries no longer in need of rediscovery once they are recorded, and transmittable to those whose ambition it is to add to them, is a great achievement of our civilization. But except in a very limited sense, it is not the kind of knowledge that is at stake in a literary education.

Those who brought English literature into the university late in the nineteenth century knew this. And lest they forget, colleagues in established fields were glad to remind them — as did the Regius Professor of Modern History at Oxford, in a broadside published in 1887 in the London *Times*:

---

1 Lionel Trilling (1905–1975), American critic, author, and teacher. Educated at Columbia University, Trilling spent much of his teaching career at Columbia. He is the author of such books as *The Liberal Imagination* (1950), *Beyond Culture: Essays on Literature and Learning* (1965), and *Sincerity and Authenticity*, and *Mind in the Modern World* (both 1972).
2 Trilling, it should be said, preferred to associate himself with the German Romantic conception of disciplined self-creation (*Bildung*), rather than with the American version of ecstatic self-discovery.
3 The phrase comes from Daniel Coit Gilman (quoted in Gerald Graff, *Professing Literature: An Institutional History*, University of Chicago Press, 1987, p. 57), the first president of the first genuine research university in the United States, Johns Hopkins.

> There are many things fit for a man's personal study, which are not fit for University examinations. One of these is "literature." ... [We are told] that it "cultivates the taste, educates the sympathies, enlarges the mind." Excellent results against which no one has a word to say. Only we cannot examine in tastes and sympathies.

English, in other words, amounted to nothing more than "chatter about Shelley."

One way some English professors defended themselves against this sort of attack was to stick to the business of establishing dates, allusions, and the historically contingent meanings of words — the sort of foundational work that had previously been done for the Greek and Roman classics. In the stringent form of philology, this was the tactic by which English teachers managed to make room for themselves in the university in the first place — though the status of philology as empirical knowledge was never entirely secure. Kernan tells how, as a student at Oxford after the war, he was trying without much success to master the history of the English language until his tutor took pity on him and advised, "When you hit a word in a text that you cannot identify, simply correlate it with some modern word that it sounds like and then invent a bridge between them. Most of the examiners will be suspicious, but may consider, so imprecise is linguistic science, your little word history an interesting possibility."

Since then, literary "science" has yielded many genuine discoveries. Biographical scholars have uncovered salient facts about authors' lives; textual scholars have hunted down corruptions introduced by copyists, printers, or intrusive editors into what authors originally wrote. But for most students, especially undergraduates, the appeal of English has never had much to do with its scholarly objectives. Students who turn with real engagement to English do so almost always because they have had the mysterious and irreducibly private experience — or at least some intimation of it — of receiving from a work of literature "an untranslatable order of impressions" that has led to "consummate moments" in which thought and feeling are fused and lifted to a new intensity. These ecstatic phrases describing aesthetic experience come from Walter Pater[1], who was writing in Oxford in the 1870s — at just that "point of English history," as T.S. Eliot[2] put it, marked by "the repudiation of revealed religion by men of culture." This was also the moment when English first entered the university as a subject of formal study.

The idea that reading can be a revelatory experience stretches back in its specifically Christian form at least to Saint Augustine[3], who wrote of being "dissociated from myself"[4] until he heard a child's voice beckoning him to open the Gospels, "repeating over and over, 'Pick up and read, pick up and read.'"

A millennium and a half later, Matthew Arnold[5] wrote in the same spirit when he defined culture (in a phrase that has often been misconstrued and

---

1 Walter Pater (1839–1894), English critic, essayist, and humanist whose advocacy of "art for art's sake" became a cardinal doctrine of the movement known as Aestheticism.

2 T. S. Eliot (1888–1965), American-English poet, playwright, literary critic, and editor, a leader of the modernist movement in poetry in such works as *The Waste Land* (1922) and *Four Quartets* (1943). Eliot exercised a strong influence on Anglo-American culture from the 1920s until late in the century.

3 Saint Augustine (354–430), bishop of Hippo from 396 to 430, one of the Latin Fathers of the Church, one of the Doctors of the Church, and perhaps the most significant Christian thinker after St. Paul. Augustine's adaptation of classical thought to Christian teaching created a theological system of great power and lasting influence. His numerous written works, the most important of which are *Confessions* and *City of God*, shaped the practice of biblical exegesis and helped lay the foundation for much of medieval and modern Christian thought. This, however, should not be confused with the Italian missionary, often known as Saint Augustine of Canterbury, who was sent by Pope St. Gregory I in 597 to convert the English to Christianity.

4 This is Henry Chadwick's recent translation of Augustine's phrase "*Ideo ... dissipabar a me ipso.*"

5 Matthew Arnold (1822–1888), English Victorian poet and literary and social critic, best known for his major work *Culture and Anarchy*.

misappropriated) as the "pursuit of total perfection by means of getting to know ... the best which has been thought and said in the world, and through this knowledge, turning a stream of fresh and free thought upon our stock notions and habits." For Augustine, "the best which has been thought and said" was to be found exclusively in scripture; for Arnold, it was more various — scattered throughout all works capable of leading readers beyond the "bounded intellectual horizon within which we have long lived."

Like any religion that has been codified and institutionalized, this "religion of culture" (as Arnold's detractors called it) has been susceptible to deformations — proselytizing the impressionable young, degenerating into idolatry, clinging to rituals long after the spirit from which they originally arose is attenuated or gone. Yet something like faith in the transforming power of literature is surely requisite for the teacher who would teach with passion and conviction. It is a faith expressed uncommonly well by Emerson some thirty years before Arnold:

> Literature is a point outside of our hodiernal[1] circle through which a new one may be described. The use of literature is to afford us a platform whence we may command a view of our present life, a purchase by which we may move it.

This large assertion links aesthetic response with moral (or what Kernan prefers to call "existential") knowledge, and even with the imperative to take reformist action in the world. For Arnold, culture had nothing to do with the motive "to plume" oneself with "a smattering of Greek and Latin," or to wear one's education as a "badge" of social distinction. To acquire culture was, instead, to become aware of the past and restless with complacencies of the present, and to be stirred by the "aspiration to leave the world better and happier than we found it." As long as teachers of literature acknowledged

---

1 Of or pertaining to the present day.

their responsibility for transmitting culture in this sense, they held a dignified position in the university. In fact, since the decline of classics and theology, and the takeover of philosophy departments by technical analytic philosophers, they have stood, along with those historians who continue to practice narrative and cultural history in the grand nineteenth-century style, as the last caretakers of the Arnoldian tradition.

Today, when students are more and more focused, as Scholes puts it, on acquiring "technological truth in the form of engineering, computer science, biotechnology, and applications of physics and chemistry," the university's obligation is surely larger than ever to see that students encounter works of literature in which the human "truths" they bring with them to college are questioned and tested. There is no inviolable reason why this sort of education must proceed chiefly in the English department; and to some extent it has already migrated at some institutions into "core curricula" where the Jewish and Christian Bibles and Greek and Roman classics are read in translation (inevitably at some loss), along with later works of philosophy and history. But for the foreseeable future, the English department will remain a main source and training ground for most college teachers of literature, and the condition of the English department is a pretty reliable measure of the state of liberal education in general.

Kernan gives a moving account of how he taught Aeschylus' *Oresteia*[1] (in Richmond Lattimore's translation) in a "Great Books" course at Yale — with a teaching method that runs close to the pulpit technique of "opening" the text and that accords with Arnold's idea of what culture should mean:

> I analyzed the trilogy in a formalist manner, mainly following a scenic and imagery pattern in which again and again light and hope flare up, only to expire in darkness and despair, and then to be relit once more. A play that

---

1 For more on this trilogy see supplementary information.

begins in darkness lit by the small, distant fire announcing the fall of Troy ends at last in the full blaze of noon of the Athenian theater and the Athenian court. I did not hesitate to point out to the students that the struggle for justice that is Aeschylus's subject is still played out every day in our courts, where rational laws free murderers because there is a shred of reasonable doubt, and the families of the murdered cry out and demand what we have come to call "victim's rights." This, I told them, or most often tried to extract from them in discussion, without apology for connecting literature with life, is where the real power of great literature lies, in its ability to portray feelingly and convincingly critical human concerns in terms that do not scant its full human reality and its desperate importance to our lives. All the aesthetic formalist aspects of the play — Aeschylus's extraordinarily tangled language, the profusion of imagery, the repetitive hope-failure pattern of the plot, the intense and brooding characters — were, in my opinion, ultimately in the service of the play's presentation of the human need for full justice and explanation of why it is so difficult to achieve. I was not arguing that the play has a "message," that it carries some social argument for a better court system; rather, it offers a universal description of where we humans live always in relation to justice. This is, I suppose, a view of the purpose of art that would most readily be called "moral," and I would not repudiate the term entirely, but I think that "existential" would be a far better term, for "moral" carries with it the suggestion of some rigid prescription, of a limited and coercive point of view, which is not the way great literature works.

This way of teaching may strike the resolute historical scholar as too "presentist," and the present-minded theorist as too "universalist." But these objections will never vitiate the gratitude of a student who has been touched by such a teacher.

The sad news is that teachers of literature have lost faith in their subject and in themselves. "We are in trouble," as Scholes puts it, "precisely because we have allowed ourselves to be persuaded that we cannot make truth claims but must go on 'professing' just the same." But what kind of dubious "truth-claims" does literature make? Literature does not embody, as both outraged conservatives and radical debunkers would have it, putatively eternal values that its professors are sworn to defend. It does not transmit moral certainty so much as record moral conflict. Its only unchanging "truth-claim" is that experience demands self-questioning.

"Literature," as Carl Woodring puts it with typical understatement, "is useful for a skeptical conduct of life." If the English department becomes permanently marginal, students will have been cheated and the university left without a moral center. This is why the state of literary studies is a problem not just for literature professors, but for everyone.[1]

I. Supplementary information

1. *Oresteia*

Oresteia, trilogy of tragic dramas by the ancient Greek dramatist Aeschylus, first performed in 458 BCE. It is his last work and the only complete trilogy of Greek dramas that has survived. *The Oresteia* tells the story of the house of Atreus. The first play, *Agamemnon*, portrays the victorious return of that king from the Trojan War and his murder by his

---

[1] Some educational leaders are showing concern that this may be happening, including the president of Harvard, Neil Rudenstine, whose degree was in English, and who devoted his 1998 commencement address to a defense of the humanities as "essential ... to any serious definition of education" — a statement that, by the felt need to make it, constitutes a noteworthy alarm. Harvard, after all, was founded by clergymen who "dread[ed] to leave an illiterate Ministry to the Churches, when our present Ministers shall lie in the Dust."

wife, Clytemnestra, and her lover, Aegisthus. The second play, *Choephoroi* (The Libation Bearers), deals with Agamemno's daughter Electra and his son Orestes. Orestes avenges his father's murder by killing his mother and her lover. The third play, *Eumenides*, describes Orestes driven by the Furies (Erinyes), for, though he was required to avenge his father's death, a matricide is infamous in the eyes of the gods. He is finally absolved at the court of the Areopagus by the goddess Athena (Britannica).

2. History of English as a Discipline[1]

The history of English as a discipline to be taught in schools and universities coincides with the history of how literature came to be valued as something worth teaching.

In the English-speaking world, the rise of literature began in 18th-century England. In this period literature became dislocated from everyday social life. As literature (along with art) became a discrete entity that was no longer woven into social relations but seen as a separate thing or isolatable experience, it became capable of being analysed and given a raised status. This was also the rise of "aesthetics."

By the 19th century, other factors contributed to bringing English into academia. The single most important influence favouring the growth of English studies was the failure of religion. Also, while English was not a direct substitute for religion, it held a remarkably similar discourse. Like religion, it was capable of operating at every social level, and it had a pacifying influence. George Gordon, an early Professor of English Literature at Oxford said at this time: "England is sick, and English literature must save it. The Churches (as I understand) having failed, and social remedies being slow, English literature has now a triple function: still, I suppose, to delight and instruct us, but also, and above all, to save our souls and heal the State".

---

1 From "The Academy" by ACU National with minor editing.

Therefore, literature was called into a kind of national service to mend the cracks that religion had left. It was to do this by its appeal to all social classes. English was to be taught because, as a Victorian handbook for English teachers put it, it helps to "promote sympathy and fellow feeling among all classes." It was thought that it also had the power to elevate the minds of the lower classes. It would communicate to them the moral riches of bourgeois civilisation, impress upon them a reverence for middle-class achievements, and, since reading is an essentially solitary, contemplative activity, curb in them any disruptive tendency to collective political action. Like religion, literature works primarily by emotion and experience, and so was well-fitted to carry through the ideological task which religion left off. The "experience" of literature is not only the homeland of ideology, but also in its literary form a kind of vicarious self-fulfillment. If you cannot experience living on a vast estate with a house full of servants, you can at least read about it.

It is for all these reasons that English as an academic subject was first institutionalised not in the universities, but in the Mechanics' Institutes and working men's colleges. English was literally the poor man's Classics, a way of providing an education for those who would never attend public schools and Oxford or Cambridge. The emphasis within English studies was on solidarity between the social classes, national pride, and moral values. It is noteworthy that the lower classes rather than the educated ones were being instructed in class solidarity. Apparently English literature was entrusted with the task of preventing social unrest.

The rise of English in England is also parallel to the admission of women into higher education. Because English is concerned with "feeling and experience", it was deemed suitable for the improvement of women, who were excluded from science and the professions. Ironically, when English came to be taught in the universities, Sir Arthur Quiller Couch, the first Professor of English at Cambridge University, would open with the word

"Gentlemen" lectures addressed to a hall filled largely with women.

While English was slow to make it to Oxford and Cambridge, it really came into its own as a discipline after World War I, led by people like F.R. Leavis (who had a background in history) and later Q.D. Leavis (who was from psychology and cultural anthropology). They led a new movement that changed the way English studies were viewed. English was suddenly in vogue as an intellectual pursuit due largely to the efforts of the Leavises. In a matter of a few decades, English went from a field with questionable legitimacy and an uncertain future to (in Terry Eagleton's words) an arena in which the most fundamental questions of human existence — what it meant to be a person, to engage in significant relationships with others, to live from the vital centre of the most essential values — were thrown into vivid relief and made the object of the most intensive scrutiny. By the late 1920s and early 1930s, English was a central subject at Cambridge, superior to law, science, politics, philosophy or history.

English as a discipline continued to flourish. From the 1930s to the 1950s American New Criticism was making its mark with the work of T.S. Eliot, I.A. Richards and W.K. Wimsatt. From this point onwards, the major changes in English were within the discipline itself in the form of changes and shifts in literary theory and approaches. The 1970s brought a challenge as to whether literature could encompass the universal values espoused by the Leavises, which led to a splintering of multiple perspectives and approaches. Marxism came and went, and feminism provided a major shot in the arm for literary studies and has remained a lasting influence. The 1980s saw the arrival of multiculturalism, and other -isms continued into the 1990s: post-structuralism, post-modernism, post-colonialism.

In the 21st century, English and the humanities are in the position of justifying their existence in universities and proving their worth in an environment that equates the university with the "marketplace". We find ourselves in the position of arguing all over again why literature and English studies matter. With an emphasis now on vocational subjects, English is once again seen as something of a "soft" option. Looking at the history of English studies, we see that it is a complex and intellectually demanding discipline that has a place beyond the "marketplace".

II. Questions to think about as you read the text

1. The author makes a distinction between the existential and moral in the discussion. But in what way are they also connected as far as literature is concerned?
2. Is Arnold justified in finding in literature a substitute for the declining religion?

III. Suggested essay topics

1. Write an essay on how a literary work changed you in some way.
2. The use of literature in a technology-driven age.

IV. Further reading

Literature, Science, and Democracy[1]

    The axioms of democracy — the doctrines of the supremacy of the individual, of the equality of men, and of man's freedom and responsibility — are derived from insight, and cannot be verified by external measurements. Unfortunately, those of us who wish to defend these axioms are handicapped by the fact that our culture is out of balance. Its respect for science is one of its glories, but its lack of respect for literature is a grave error of judgment. Why is our culture out of balance? Why do we respect objectivity only and neglect insight? Why do we regard science as a necessity and literature as a

---

1 From Henry Myers, *The Pacific Spectator*, Volume VIIII, No. 4, Autumn, 1954.

luxury?

One reason is that we are in a period of reaction against excessive claims made in the past for poetry and poetic intuition. After Immanuel Kant[1] had apparently shown, late in the eighteenth century, that scientific reason falls into hopeless contradiction when it is applied to such questions as the existence of God and the immortality of the soul, poets were encouraged to answer transcendental questions on intuitive grounds. Wordsworth[2] feels the presence of God in nature, and has intuitive intimations of immortality. Whitman tells us again and again that he knows he is immortal. Tennyson[3] speaks with final confidence of

> One God, one law, one element,
> And one far-off divine event,
> To which the whole creation moves.

We respect these convictions as evidences of faith, but we have every reason to believe that the intuitions upon which the nineteenth-century poets and prophets relied cannot be empirically verified. Although literature adequately reveals the hopes and fears, and the doubts and beliefs of men concerning things beyond our present experience, literature as such cannot turn faith into certainty. Those who insist, for example, that the Bible is only great literature must look elsewhere for certainty about the supernatural; and

---

1 Immanuel Kant (1724–1804), German philosopher whose comprehensive and systematic work in the theory of knowledge, ethics, and aesthetics greatly influenced all subsequent philosophy. His major works are *Critique of Pure Reason*, *Critique of Practical Reason* and *Critique of Judgment*.
2 William Wordsworth (1770–1850), major English poet of the Romantic period, whose *Lyrical Ballads* (1798), written in cooperation with Samuel Taylor Coleridge, helped launch this literary movement in England.
3 Lord Alfred Tennyson (1809–1892), English poet often regarded as the chief representative of the Victorian age in poetry.

those who accept the Bible as divinely inspired are relying on a power far beyond the natural powers of the poet. Few people today would agree with Matthew Arnold, who believed that poetry will replace theology and the poet replace the theologian. T. S. Eliot is much closer to the truth in maintaining that nothing can ever be a satisfactory substitute for something else.

The poetic insight which I have been describing as the essence of literature is altogether different from the intuition of the nineteenth-century prophet. The prophet's intuitions about the transcendental and the supernatural cannot be demonstrated, and, without the support of faith, must always remain conjectural; the poet's insights into present experience, however, may be demonstrated and may be tested by further experience and shown to be either true or false.

Most present-day critics and poets, in their reaction against the exaggerated claims made for prophetic intuition, have unfortunately gone to the other extreme. For them poetry is a purely aesthetic experience which has little or nothing to do with either meaning or morality. To go to this extreme is to throw out the baby with the bath water. Although we must reject the prophet's claim that, through intuition, he can offer us assurances about God and the hereafter, we should recognize that the poet, if he is gifted with insight, is a trustworthy observer of the life of man here and now.

A second reason for our failure to understand the nature and function of literature is the old but as yet unexploded notion that there can be only one trustworthy source of knowledge. Poets, philosophers, rhetoricians, theologians, and scientists of many varieties, exact and social, have too often been rivals rather than collaborators in the pursuit of knowledge. Each has at some time or other sought recognition as the only reliable teacher. This rivalry, which arises from the natural tendency of every man to overestimate the worth of what he knows best, or can do best, can be traced from its beginnings in Plato's attack on the poets through the attack on the philosophers by the rhetoricians, Isocrates[1] and Quintilian[2], and on up to the present time. A wise man, after judiciously weighing the claims of each of the rivals, might well conclude that each has had, and still has, something valuable to contribute. Unfortunately, however, our age still honors the notion that there is only one trustworthy source of knowledge. The present-day form of this notion is a vague but widespread popular faith that statistics and other forms of external measurement will soon place poetry, metaphysics, theology, rhetoric, and ethics in a class with alchemy and astrology. Our age might well be called the Age of the Apotheosis of Objectivity.

The main reason why our culture is out of balance is, of course, that we have failed to understand the true nature and social function of literature. The burden of the problem of restoring the cultural balance falls largely on interpreters of literature — on critics, scholars, and teachers, who should, I believe, devote a little less time to purely aesthetic and technical studies, to the elucidation of puzzling texts, and to literary history, and a little more time to the heart of literature — insight.

Our generation has been so deeply impressed by the great achievements of scientists and technicians that it has forgotten the indispensable contributions of poets and artists. It is the special duty of a professor of literature to remind it that the axioms of democracy are derived from insight, and that sympathetic insight, the ability of one man to take another man's point of view, is and always will be, the only cement which can hold a free society together.

An ideal democratic culture depends upon our realization that the views of man afforded by literature and by science are complementary,

---

1 Isocrates (436–338BCE), ancient Athenian orator, rhetorician (rhetoric), and teacher whose writings are an important historical source on the intellectual and political life of the Athens of his day.
2 Marcus Fabius Quintilianus (35–96), Latin teacher and writer whose work on rhetoric, *Institutio oratoria*, is a major contribution to educational theory and literary criticism.

not contradictory, and that only by combining these views can we hope to come close to the full truth about ourselves. In a progressive and successful democracy man must be weighed and measured by science as well as esteemed through insight.

As the poets proclaim, man has significance and dignity — that is, he has a value beyond measuring; but, as the scientists point out, he is also a relatively weak and insignificant being, who must measure his strength carefully before judging the feasibility of any enterprise. Man is a free and responsible being, but his freedom and responsibility are limited by heredity, by environment, by capacities and incapacities which we must carefully measure if we are to reward or punish him justly for his actions. All men are equal in human worth and in the kinship of a common fate, but they are unequal in every other respect, and only by careful measuring and testing can we help each individual to find the place in society in which he can do his best.

In these ways, the poet and the scientist, properly understood, are always at work, each contributing his indispensable share to the building of our society and the perfection of our democratic justice. Indeed, the poet and the scientist are not rivals but equal and trustworthy partners in the greatest of all tasks, the task of teaching man through insight to see others as he sees himself and through objectivity to see himself as others see him.

Courtly Love[1]

Everyone has heard of courtly love, and everyone knows that it appears quite suddenly at the end of the eleventh century in Languedoc. The characteristics of the Troubadour poetry have been repeatedly described. With the form, which is lyrical, and the style, which is sophisticated and often "aureate" or deliberately enigmatic, we need not concern ourselves. The sentiment, of course, is love, but love of a highly specialized sort, whose characteristics may be enumerated as Humility, Courtesy, Adultery, and the Religion of Love. The lover is always abject. Obedience to his lady's lightest wish, however whimsical, and silent acquiescence in her rebukes, however unjust, are the only virtues he dares to claim. There is a service of love closely modelled on the service which a feudal vassal owes to his lord. The lover is the lady's "man". He addresses her as midons,[2] which etymologically represents not "my lady" but "my lord". The whole attitude has been rightly described as "a feudalisation of love". This solemn amatory ritual is felt to be part and parcel of the courtly life. It is possible only to those who are, in

---

1 Excerpted from C. S. Lewis, *The Allegory of Love: A Study in Medieval Tradition* (Oxford University Press, 1958), pp. 2–21.
2 Old French, meaning "lord" or "master." In medieval literature, "midon" was used to address or refer to noble or important figures.

the old sense of the word, polite. It thus becomes, from one point of view the flower, from another the seed, of all those noble usages which distinguish the gentle from the vilein: only the courteous can love, but it is love that makes them courteous. Yet this love, though neither playful nor licentious in its expression, is always what the nineteenth century called "dishonourable" love. The poet normally addresses another man's wife, and the situation is so carelessly accepted that he seldom concerns himself much with her husband: his real enemy is the rival. But if he is ethically careless, he is no light-hearted gallant: his love is represented as a despairing and tragical emotion — or almost despairing, for he is saved from complete wanhope[1] by his faith in the God of Love who never betrays his faithful worshippers and who can subjugate the cruellest beauties.

The characteristics of this sentiment, and its systematic coherence throughout the love poetry of the Troubadours as a whole, are so striking that they easily lead to a fatal misunderstanding. We are tempted to treat "courtly love" as a mere episode in literary history — an episode that we have finished with as we have finished with the peculiarities of Skaldic verse or Euphuistic prose. In fact, however, an unmistakable continuity connects the Provençal love song with the love poetry of the later Middle Ages, and thence, through Petrarch and many others, with that of the present day. If the thing at first escapes our notice, this is because we are so familiar with the erotic tradition of modern Europe that we mistake it for something natural and universal and therefore do not inquire into its origins. It seems to us natural that love should be the commonest theme of serious imaginative literature: but a glance at classical antiquity or at the Dark Ages at once shows us that what we took for "nature" is really a special state of affairs, which will probably have an end, and which certainly had a beginning in eleventh-century Provence. It seems — or it seemed to us till lately — a natural thing that love (under

---

1 An archaic word meaning despair or hopelessness.

certain conditions) should be regarded as a noble and ennobling passion: it is only if we imagine ourselves trying to explain this doctrine to Aristotle, Virgil, St. Paul, or the author of *Beowulf*, that we become aware how far from natural it is. Even our code of etiquette, with its rule that women always have precedence, is a legacy from courtly love, and is felt to be far from natural in modern Japan or India. Many of the features of this sentiment, as it was known to the Troubadours, have indeed disappeared; but this must not blind us to the fact that the most momentous and the most revolutionary elements in it have made the background of European literature for eight hundred years. French poets, in the eleventh century, discovered or invented, or were the first to express, that romantic species of passion which English poets were still writing about in the nineteenth. They effected a change which has left no corner of our ethics, our imagination, or our daily life untouched, and they erected impassable barriers between us and the classical past or the Oriental present. Compared with this revolution the Renaissance is a mere ripple on the surface of literature.

There can be no mistake about the novelty of romantic love: our only difficulty is to imagine in all its bareness the mental world that existed before its coming — to wipe out of our minds, for a moment, nearly all that makes the food both of modern sentimentality and modern cynicism ... In ancient literature love seldom rises above the levels of merry sensuality or domestic comfort, except to be treated as a tragic madness ... which plunges otherwise sane people (usually women) into crime and disgrace. Such is the love of Medea, of Phaedra, of Dido; and such the love from which maidens pray that the gods may protect them. At the other end of the scale we find the comfort and utility of a good wife acknowledged: Odysseus loves Penelope as he loves the rest of his home and possessions, and Aristotle rather grudgingly admits that the conjugal relation may now and then rise to the same level as the virtuous friendship between good men. But this has plainly very little to do with "love" in the modern or medieval sense ...

The fall of the old civilization and the coming of Christianity did not result in any deepening or idealizing of the conception of love. The fact is important, because it refutes two theories which trace the great change in our sentiments respectively to the Germanic temperament and to the Christian religion — especially to the cult of the Blessed Virgin ... But there is no evidence that the quasi-religious tone of medieval love poetry has been transferred from the worship of the Blessed Virgin: it is just as likely — it is even more likely — that the colouring of certain hymns to the Virgin has been borrowed from the love poetry. Nor is it true in any unequivocal sense that the medieval church encouraged reverence for women at all: while it is a ludicrous error to suppose that she regarded sexual passion, under any conditions or after any possible process of refinement, as a noble emotion. The other theory turns on a supposedly innate characteristic in the Germanic races, noted by Tacitus. But what Tacitus describes is a primitive awe of women as uncanny and probably prophetic beings, which is as remote from our comprehension as the primitive reverence for lunacy or the primitive horror of twins; and because it is thus remote, we cannot judge how probably it might have developed into the medieval *Frauendienst*,[1] the service of ladies. What is certain is that where a Germanic race reached its maturity untouched by the Latin spirit, as in Iceland, we find nothing at all like courtly love ...

... It is certain that the efforts of scholars have so far failed to find an origin for the content of Provençal love poetry. Celtic, Byzantine, and even Arabic influence have been suspected; but it has not been made clear that these, if granted, could account for the results we see ... Something can be extracted from a study of the social conditions in which the new poetry arose, but not

---

1 German. In medieval literature and chivalric traditions, this word referred to the acts of devotion, honor, and service performed by knights or men toward women, particularly noble or high-ranking ladies.

so much as we might hope. We know that the crusading armies thought the Provençals milksops, but this will seem relevant only to a very hardened enemy of *Frauendienst*. We know that this period in the south of France had witnessed what seemed to contemporaries a signal degeneracy from the simplicity of ancient manners and an alarming increase of luxury ... Much more important is the fact that landless knighthood — knighthood without a place in the territorial hierarchy of feudalism — seems to have been possible in Provence. The unattached knight, as we meet him in the romances, respectable only by his own valour, amiable only by his own courtesy, predestined lover of other men's wives, was therefore a reality; but this does not explain why he loved in such a new way. If courtly love necessitates adultery, adultery hardly necessitates courtly love. We come much nearer to the secret if we can accept the picture of a typical Provençal court drawn many years ago by an English writer, and since approved by the greatest living authority on the subject. We must picture a castle which is a little island of comparative leisure and luxury, and therefore at least of possible refinement, in a barbarous country-side. There are many men in it, and very few women — the lady, and her damsels. Around these throng the whole male *meiny* (retinue), the inferior nobles, the landless knights, the squires, and the pages — haughty creatures enough in relation to the peasantry beyond the walls, but feudally inferior to the lady as to her lord — her "men" as feudal language had it. Whatever "courtesy" is in the place flows from her: all female charm from her and her damsels. There is no question of marriage for most of the court. All these circumstances together come very near to being a "cause"; but they do not explain why very similar conditions elsewhere had to wait for Provençal example before they produced like results. Some part of the mystery remains inviolate.

But if we abandon the attempt to explain the new feeling, we can at least explain ... the peculiar form which it first took; the four marks of Humility, Courtesy, Adultery, and the Religion of Love. To account for the humility we need no more than has already been said. Before the coming of courtly love the relation of vassal and lord, in all its intensity and warmth, already existed; it was a mould into which romantic passion would almost certainly be poured. And if the beloved were also the feudal superior the thing becomes entirely natural and inevitable. The emphasis on courtesy results from the same conditions. It is in courts that the new feeling arises: the lady, by her social and feudal position, is already the arbitress of manners and the scourge of "villany" even before she is loved. The association of love with adultery — an association which has lasted in continental literature down to our own times — has deeper causes. In part, it can be explained by the picture we have already drawn; but there is much more to be said about it than this. Two things prevented the men of that age from connecting their ideal of romantic and passionate love with marriage.

The first is, of course, the actual practice of feudal society. Marriages had nothing to do with love, and no "nonsense" about marriage was tolerated. All matches were matches of interest, and, worse still, of an interest that was continually changing. When the alliance which had answered would answer no longer, the husband's object was to get rid of the lady as quickly as possible. Marriages were frequently dissolved. The same woman who was the lady and "the dearest dread" of her vassals was often little better than a piece of property to her husband. He was master in his own house. So far from being a natural channel for the new kind of love, marriage was rather the drab background against which that love stood out in all the contrast of its new tenderness and delicacy. The situation is indeed a very simple one, and not peculiar to the Middle Ages. Any idealization of sexual love, in a society where marriage is purely utilitarian, must begin by being an idealization of adultery.

The second factor is the medieval theory of marriage — what may be called, by a convenient modern barbarism, the "sexology" of the medieval church. A nineteenth century Englishman felt that the same passion — romantic love — could be either virtuous or vicious according as it was directed towards marriage or not. But according to the medieval view passionate love itself was wicked, and did not cease to be wicked if the object of it were your wife. If a man had once yielded to this emotion, he had no choice between "guilty" and "innocent" love before him: he had only the choice, either of repentance, or else of different forms of guilt ... [1]

It will be seen that the medieval theory finds room for innocent sexuality: what it does not find room for is passion, whether romantic or otherwise. It might almost be said that it denies to passion the indulgence which it reluctantly accords to appetite ...

Finally we come to the fourth mark of courtly love — its love religion of the god Amor. This is partly, as we have seen, an inheritance from Ovid. [2] In part it is due to that same law of transference which determined that all the emotion stored in the vassal's relation to his *seigneur* should attach itself to the new kind of love: the forms of religious emotion would naturally tend to get into the love poetry, for the same reason. But in part this erotic religion arises as a rival or a parody of the real religion and emphasizes the antagonism of the two ideals ...

... [In a twelfth-century poem] the French poet has taken over this conception of an erotic religion with a full understanding of its flippancy, and proceeded to elaborate the joke in terms of the only religion he knows — medieval Christianity. The result is a close and impudent parody of the practices of the Church, in which Ovid becomes a *doctor egregius* (eminent doctor) and

---

1   In the following paragraph, which is omitted here, C. S. Lewis provides an overview of the medieval understanding of marriage, desire, and pleasure within the context of Christian beliefs and the Fall. He surveys the perspectives of various medieval churchmen on the sexual act within marriage. While some believed that the desire and pleasure associated with it were morally evil, others argued that they were not sinful but a result of the Fall. For still others, even passionate love for one's own wife is considered adultery.

2   Publius Ovidius Naso (43 BCE–18 CE), Roman poet, author of *Metamorphoses*, *Amores* (Loves), *Epistulea Herodium* (Letters from Heroines) and *Ars Amatoria* (The Art of Love). The last contains instructions on how to acquire and keep a lover.

the *Ars Amatoria* (*The Art of Love*) a gospel, erotic heterodoxy and orthodoxy are distinguished, and the god of Love is equipped with cardinals and exercises the power of excommunication. The Ovidian tradition, operated upon by the medieval taste for humorous blasphemy, is apparently quite sufficient to produce a love religion, and even in a sense a Christianized love religion, without any aid from the new seriousness of romantic passion. As against any theory which would derive medieval *Frauendienst* from Christianity and the worship of the Blessed Virgin, we must insist that the love religion often begins as a parody of the real religion ...

I. Supplementary information

1. The Middle Ages

The Middle Ages refers to the period in European history from the collapse of Roman civilization in Western Europe in the 5th century to the period of the Renaissance. The term was coined by Italian humanists of the latter period who were engaged in a revival of classical learning and culture. Although Western civilization did shift to a low gear in the Middle Ages, the notion of a thousand-year period of darkness and ignorance separating the Renaissance from the ancient Greek and Roman world, was very much the invention of these scholars and artists to serve the purpose of highlighting their own work and ideals. One of the most important features of the Middle Ages was the ascendancy of Christianity.

2. Courtly love

Courtly love, a concept that emerged in medieval Europe, represents a distinctive form of romantic devotion that transcended the bounds of marriage and celebrated the idealized love between a knight and a noblewoman. Originating in the noble courts of the 12th century, courtly love encompassed a set of conventions, rituals, and literary themes that shaped the expression of love and desire. Central to this notion was the idea of chivalry, with knights professing their unwavering devotion, engaging in acts of service, and expressing their feelings through refined language and gestures. Courtly love idealized the beloved lady as an object of adoration, inspiring poets and troubadours to compose lyrical verses and songs that elevated her to the realm of divine beauty. While courtly love existed within the confines of an established social hierarchy, it provided an outlet for the expression of intense emotions and set the stage for the development of poetic and literary traditions that continue to captivate and inspire to this day.

II. Questions to think about as you read the text

1. Of the several explanations of the origin of courtly love, which one is most plausible, even though Lewis finds none satisfactory?
2. If courtly love was adulterous by nature, what elements of medieval culture served to justify its existence?

III. Suggested essay topics

1. Write an essay commenting on medieval courtly love from a feminist perspective.
2. The Middle Ages, for all its supposed darkness, has been attractive in various ways to people of subsequent ages. Write an essay on its attractions to someone in the 21st century.

IV. Further reading

The Medieval Social Order: A Human Body Analogy

The medieval era, spanning from the 5th to the 15th century, was characterized by a hierarchical social structure known as the feudal system. An intriguing aspect of this system was the analogy drawn between the human body and the different social classes. Knowledge about the medieval social order and the symbolism behind the human body analogy enables us to understand the interconnectedness and interdependence of the various strata of society.

The Head: the Nobility and Monarchy

At the top of the medieval social order stood the nobility, analogous to the head of the human body. Just as the head guides and governs the body, the nobility held power and authority over the realm. They included kings, queens, dukes, and other high-ranking aristocrats who enjoyed privileges, controlled land, and possessed military might. Their role was to provide leadership and protection to the rest of society.

The Arms: Military and Clergy

The arms, symbolizing the military and the clergy, occupied the next position in the medieval social hierarchy. The military class, including knights and warriors, acted as the defense system of the society, protecting the realm from external threats. Similarly, the clergy, comprising bishops, priests, and monks, safeguarded the spiritual well-being of the population. Both the arms and the clergy played vital roles in maintaining stability and order.

The Torso: The Bourgeoisie and Peasantry

Analogous to the torso, the middle strata of medieval society consisted of the bourgeoisie and the peasantry. The bourgeoisie, or the merchant class, formed the economic backbone of the society. They engaged in trade, commerce, and finance, contributing to the growth of towns and cities. On the other hand, the peasantry, comprising farmers, laborers, and serfs, toiled on the land, producing essential goods for sustenance and the overall economy. Together, they provided the necessary sustenance and resources for the social order.

The Legs: Serfs and Unskilled Laborers

At the bottom of the medieval social order were the serfs and unskilled laborers, represented by the legs of the human body. Serfs were tied to the land and worked for their lord in exchange for protection and a share of the produce. They formed the backbone of agricultural labor. Unskilled laborers, including servants and apprentices, contributed to various sectors but had limited social mobility. The legs symbolized the foundation upon which the entire social structure stood.

The medieval social order, represented in terms of the human body, provided a framework to understand the interdependence and hierarchical structure prevalent in that era. Each social class played a crucial role, just as each part of the body has its own function in maintaining overall health. Although this system may seem rigid and unequal by modern standards, it shaped the socio-political landscape of the time and laid the foundation for future societal developments. Exploring the medieval social order through the lens of the human body analogy enriches our understanding of the complexities of the era.

What Is Humanism?[1]

...

We should of course remember that though we have been talking of ancient humanism and humanists, the word humanist was not used until the Renaissance and the word humanism not until a still later period. In studying the humanism of the Renaissance the significant contrast that we need to note is the one commonly made at this time between humanity and divinity. In its essence the Renaissance is a protest against the time when there was too much divinity and not enough humanity, against the starving and stunting of certain sides of man by mediaeval theology, against a vision of the supernatural that imposed a mortal constraint upon his more purely human and natural faculties. The models of a full and free play of these faculties were sought in the ancient classics, but the cult of the ancients soon became itself a superstition, so that a man was called a humanist from the mere fact of having received an initiation into the ancient languages, even though he had little or nothing of the doctrine and discipline that the term should imply. Very few of the early

---

1 From Chapter One of *Literature and the American College* (1908) by Irving Babbitt.

Italian humanists were really humane.[1] For many of them humanism, so far from being a doctrine and discipline, was a revolt from all discipline, a wild rebound from the mediaeval extreme into an opposite excess. What predominates in the first part of the Renaissance is a movement of emancipation — emancipation of the senses, of the intellect, and in the northern countries of the conscience. It was the first great modern era of expansion, the first forward push of individualism. As in all such periods, the chief stress is on the broadening of knowledge, and, so far as was compatible with the humanistic exclusiveness, of sympathy. The men of that time had what Emerson calls a canine appetite for knowledge. The ardor with which they broke away from the bonds and leading-strings of mediaeval tradition, the exuberance with which they celebrated the healing of the long feud between nature and human nature, obscured for a time the need of decorum and selection. A writer like Rabelais,[2] for instance, is neither decorous nor select; and so in spite of his great genius would probably have seemed to a cultivated ancient barbaric rather than humane. Such a disorderly and undisciplined unfolding of the faculties of the individual, such an overemphasis on the benefits of liberty as compared with the benefits of restraint, brought in its train the evils that are peculiar to periods of expansion. There was an increase in anarchical self-assertion and self-indulgence that seemed a menace to the very existence of society; and so society reacted against the individual and an era of expansion was followed by an era of concentration. This change took place at different times, and under different circumstances, in different countries. In Italy the change coincides roughly with the sack of

---

1 In an early part of this piece, not selected here, Babbitt talks about the tendency to confuse humanism with philanthropy.
2 François Rabelais (?1494–1553), French writer chiefly known for his satirical work *Gargantua and Pantagruel*.

Rome (1527)[1] and the Council of Trent[2]; in France it follows the frightful anarchy of the wars of religion and finds political expression in Henry IV, and literary expression in Malherbe.[3] Of course in so complex a period as the Renaissance we must allow for innumerable eddies and crosscurrents and for almost any number of individual exceptions. In an age as well as in an individual there are generally elements, often important elements, that run counter to the main tendency. But if one is not a German doctor who has to prove his "originality," or a lover of paradox for its own sake, it is usually possible to discern the main drift in spite of the eddies and counter-currents.

We may affirm, then, that the main drift of the later Renaissance was away from a humanism that favored a free expansion toward a humanism that was in the highest degree disciplinary and selective. The whole movement was complicated by what is at bottom a different problem, the need that was felt in France and Italy, at least, of protecting society against the individual. One can insist on selection and discipline without at the same time being so distrustful of individualism. Many of the humanists of this period fell into hardness and narrowness (in other words, ceased to be humane) from overemphasis on a discipline that was to be imposed from without and from above, and on a doctrine that was to be codified

---

1 In 1527 forces of the Holy Roman Emperor, Charles V, now dominant in Italy after defeating the French at Pavia two years before, stormed the city of Rome and starting a frenzy of devastation and carnage in the ancient capital.
2 19th ecumenical council of the Roman Catholic Church, convoked to deal with the crisis of the Protestant Reformation. The council played a vital role in revitalizing the Roman Catholic church in that the subsequent Counter Reformation was to a great extent an implementation of its principles and requirements.
3 François de Malherbe (1555–1628), French poet and critic, official poet of Henry IV and Louis XIII. Malherbe was also an influential critic, who was a staunch advocate of objectivity, precision of language, and seriousness of purpose, ideals which were soon to be associated with classicism.

in a multitude of minute prescriptions. The essence of art, according to that highly astringent genius, Scaliger, who had a European influence on the literary criticism of this age, is *electio et fastidium sui* — selection and fastidiousness toward one's self (in practice Scaliger reserved his fastidiousness for other people). This spirit of fastidious selection gained ground until, instead of the expansive Rabelais, we have the exclusive Malherbe, until a purism grew up that threatened to impoverish men's ideas and emotions as well as their vocabulary ...

The contrast between the disciplinary and selective humanism of the later Renaissance and the earlier period of expansion should not blind us to the underlying unity of aim. Like the ancient humanists whom they took as their guides, the men of both periods aimed at forming the complete man (*totus, teres atque rotundus*). But the men of the later period and the neo-classicists in general hoped to attain this completeness not so much by the virtues of expansion as by the virtues of concentration. It seemed to them that the men of the earlier period had left too much opening for the whims and vagaries of the individual; and so they were chiefly concerned with making a selection of subjects and establishing a doctrine and discipline that should be universal and human. To this end the classical doctrine and discipline were to be put into the service of the doctrine and discipline of Christianity. This attempt at a compromise between the pagan and Christian traditions is visible both in Catholic countries in the Jesuit schools, and in Protestant countries in the selection of studies that took shape in the old college curriculum. No doubt the selection of both divinity and humanity that was intended to be representative was inadequate; and no doubt the whole compromise between doctrines and disciplines, that were in many respects divergent and in some respects hostile, laid itself open to the charge of being superficial. The men of the early Renaissance had felt more acutely the antagonism between divinity as then understood and humanity, and had often taken sides uncompromisingly for one or the other. Machiavelli[1] accused Christianity of having made the world effeminate, whereas Luther looked on the study of the pagan classics, except within the narrowest bounds, as pernicious. Calvin execrated Rabelais, and Rabelais denounced Calvin as an impostor. Yet, after all, the effort to make the ancient humanities and arts of expression tributary to Christianity was in many respects admirable, and the motto that summed it up, *sapiens atque eloquens pietas* (wise and eloquent piety), might still, if properly interpreted, be used to define the purpose of the college.

I. Supplementary information

1. Irving Babbitt

Irving Babbitt, born in 1865, was an influential American literary critic and cultural philosopher of the early 20th century. Babbitt studied at Harvard University and at the Sorbonne in Paris, and was professor of French and comparative literature at Harvard from 1894 until his death in 1933. Babbitt was known for his rigorous criticism of Romanticism and its offshoots, Realism and Naturalism. In his notable book *Literature and the American College*, Babbitt challenged prevailing notions of progress and proposed a return to timeless ideals found in classical literature and philosophy. Indeed, these ideas lay at the centre of the literary and philosophical movement known as New Humanism, of which Babbitt was the leading proponent. Through his writings and teachings, Babbitt left a lasting impact on American

---

1 Niccolò Machiavelli (1469–1527), Italian political philosopher best known for his book *The Prince*, in which he advises princes on how to gain and keep power.

intellectual discourse, urging society to recognize the vital role of ethical and intellectual development in shaping individuals and fostering a healthier and more meaningful cultural life.

2. Origin and Meaning of the Term Humanism

The term humanism has its roots in the historical and intellectual context of the Renaissance period. Originally known as *"humanismus"* in the works of 19th-century German scholars, it was used to describe the Renaissance emphasis on classical studies in education. However, its origins can be traced back even further. In the late 15th century, educators known as *umanisti*, referring to professors or students of classical literature, pursued and advocated for these studies. The word *umanisti* derived from the *studia humanitatis*, a curriculum of classical studies that encompassed grammar, poetry, rhetoric, history, and moral philosophy. This curriculum was considered equivalent to the Greek *paideia* and was rooted in the Latin concept of *humanitas*, an educational and political ideal that formed the intellectual foundation of the entire humanist movement. From its humble beginnings in classical education, humanism evolved into a comprehensive reform of culture, seeking to unleash the grandest human potentialities and transform society.

II. Questions to think about as you read the text

1. Classical knowledge played dissimilar roles at different stages of the Renaissance according to Babbitt. How did its role vary?
2. If the Renaissance was initially a protest against too much divinity, why then did Christianity become useful in the later stage?

III. Suggested essay questions

1. Renaissance humanism highlights the interchangeability of what is old and what is new at least in cultural history. Write an essay on a similar

case that you are familiar with.

2. Now that you know something about both the Middle Ages and the Renaissance, write an essay on the difference in love between the two cultural periods. Illustrate your point with specific works of art or literature whenever necessary.

IV. Further reading

Following is an excerpt from Jacob Burckhardt's influential essay on the Renaissance. This work, first published in 1860, provided subsequent ages with a model for the study of cultural history.

From *The Civilization of The Renaissance in Italy*[1]

Some modern writers deplore the fact that the germs of a far more independent and essentially national culture, such as appeared in Florence about the year 1300, were afterward so completely swamped by the humanists. There was then, we are told, nobody in Florence who could not read; even the donkey men sang the verses of Dante, and the best Italian manuscripts that we possess originally belonged to Florentine artisans; the publication of a popular encyclopedia such as the *Tesoro* [*Li livres dou trésor*] of Brunetto Latini, was possible then; and all this was founded on a strength and soundness of character due to the universal participation in public affairs, to commerce and travel, and to the systematic reprobation of idleness. The Florentines were at time respected and influential throughout the whole world, and not without reason did Pope Boniface VIII in that very year call them the "the fifth element." The rapid progress of humanism after the year 1400 paralyzed native impulses. Henceforth men looked only to antiquity for the

---

1 By Jacob Burckhardt (1818–1897), translated by S.G.C. Middlemore.

solution of every problem, and consequently allowed literature to turn into mere quotation. The very fall of civil freedom is partly ascribed to all this, since the new learning rested on obedience to authority, sacrificed municipal rights to Roman law, and thereby both sought and found the favor of the despots.

These charges will occupy us now and then, when we shall attempt to reduce them to their true value and to weigh the losses against the gains. For the present we must confine ourselves to showing that the civilization of the vigorous fourteenth century necessarily prepared the way for the complete victory of humanism, and that the greatest representatives of the national Italian spirit were the very men who opened wide the gate for the measureless devotion to antiquity in the fifteenth century.

First, Dante. If a succession of men of equal genius had presided over Italian culture, whatever elements their natures might have absorbed from the antique, they still could not fail to retain a characteristic and strongly marked national stamp. But neither Italy nor Western Europe produced another Dante, and he was and remained the man who first thrust antiquity into the foreground of national culture. In the *Divine Comedy* he treats the ancient and the Christian worlds, not indeed as of equal authority, but as parallel to one another. Just as, at an earlier period of the Middle Ages, types and antitypes were sought in the history of the Old and New Testaments, so does Dante constantly bring together a Christian and a pagan illustration of the same fact. It must be remembered that the Christian cycle of history and legend was familiar, whereas the ancient was relatively unknown, was full of promise and of interest, and must necessarily have gained the upper hand in the competition for public sympathy when there was no longer a Dante to maintain the balance between the two.

Petrarch lives in the memory of most people nowadays as a great Italian poet, but among his contemporaries his fame was due more to the fact that he was a kind of living representative of antiquity, that he imitated all styles of Latin poetry, and wrote letters that, as treatises on matters of antiquarian interest, obtained a reputation which to us is unintelligible, but which is understandable in an age without handbooks.

It was the same with Boccaccio. For two centuries, when little was known of the *Decameron* north of the Alps, he was famous all over Europe simply because of his Latin compilations of mythology, geography, and biography. One of these, *De genealogia deorum*, contains in the fourteenth and fifteenth books a remarkable appendix, in which he discusses the position of the then youthful humanism with regard to his time. We must not be misled by his exclusive references to poesia, as closer observation shows that he means thereby the whole mental activity of the poet — scholars. It is this activity whose enemies he combats so vigorously: the frivolous ignoramuses who have no soul for anything but debauchery; the sophistical theologian, to whom Helicon, the Castalian fountain, and the grove of Apollo are foolishness; the greedy lawyers, to whom poetry is a superfluity, since no money can be made by it; finally (described periphrastically but recognizable enough), the mendicant friars who made free with their charges of paganism and immorality. Then follows the positive defense of poetry, the praise of poetry, and especially of the deeper and allegorical meanings that we must always attribute to it, and of that calculated obscurity which is intended to repel the dull minds of the ignorant. And finally, with a clear reference to his own scholarly work, the writer justifies the new relation in which his age stood to paganism. The case was wholly different, he pleads, when the Early Church had to fight its way among the heathen. Now — praised be Jesus Christ! — true religion is strengthened, paganism destroyed, and the victorious Church in possession of the hostile camp. It is now possible to touch and study paganism almost (*fere*) without danger. This is the same argument used in later times to defend the Renaissance.

There was, thus, a new cause in the world and a new class of men to maintain it. It is idle to ask if this cause ought not to have stopped short in its victorious advance, to have restrained itself deliberately and conceded first place to purely national elements of culture. No conviction was more firmly rooted in the popular mind than that antiquity was the greatest glory Italy possessed.

Salt[1]

"Ye are the salt of the earth."
Matthew 5:13

This figure of speech is plain and pungent. Salt is savory, purifying, preservative. It is one of those superfluities which the great French wit defined as "things that are very necessary". A bag of salt, among the barbarous tribes, was worth more than a man. The Jews prized it especially, because their religion laid particular emphasis on cleanliness, and because salt was largely used in their sacrifices.

Christ chose an image which was familiar, when He said to His disciples, "Ye are the salt of the earth." This was His conception of their mission, their influence. They were to cleanse and sweeten the world in which they lived, to keep it from decay, to give a new and more wholesome flavor to human existence. Their function was not to be passive, but active. The sphere of its action was to be this present life. There is no use in saving salt for heaven. It will not be needed there. Its mission is to permeate, season, and purify things on earth.

---

[1] Reprinted from Henry van Dyke, "Salt," *Modern Eloquence*, VII (1902): 380–90.

Men of privilege without power are waste material. Men of enlightenment without influence are the poorest kind of rubbish. Men of intellectual and moral and religious culture, who are not active forces for good in society, are not worth what it costs to produce and keep them. If they pass for Christians they are guilty of obtaining respect under false pretenses. They were meant to be the salt of the earth. And the first duty of salt is to be salty.

This is the subject on which I want to speak to you today. The saltiness of salt is the symbol of a noble, powerful, truly religious life.

You college students are men of privilege. It costs ten times as much, in labor and care and money, to bring you out where you are today, as it costs to educate the average man, and a hundred times as much as it costs to raise a boy without any education. This fact brings you face to face with a question: Are you going to be worth your salt?[1]

You have had mental training and plenty of instruction in various branches of learning. You ought to be full of intelligence. You have had moral discipline, and the influences of good example have been steadily brought to bear upon you. You ought to be full of principle. You have had religious advantages and abundant inducements to choose the better part. You ought to be full of faith. What are you going to do with your intelligence, your principle, your faith? It is your duty to make active use of them for the seasoning, the cleansing, the saving of the world. Don't be sponges. Be the salt of the earth.

Think, first, of the influence for good which men of intelligence may exercise in the world, if they will only put their culture to the right use. Half of the troubles of mankind come from ignorance, — ignorance which is systematically organized with societies for its support and newspapers for its dissemination, — ignorance which consists less in not knowing things,

---

1 *worth one's salt*: doing one's job well or deserving respect; efficient and capable. Usually with expressed or implied negative: He is not worth his salt.

than in willfully ignoring the things that are already known. There are certain physical diseases which would go out of existence in ten years if people would only remember what has been learned. There are certain political and social plagues which are propagated only in the atmosphere of shallow self-confidence and vulgar thoughtlessness. There is a yellow fever of literature specially adapted and prepared for the spread of shameless curiosity, incorrect information, and complacent idiocy among all classes of the population. Persons who fall under the influence of this pest become so triumphantly ignorant that they cannot distinguish between news and knowledge. They develop a morbid thirst for printed matter, and the more they read the less they learn. They are fit soil for the bacteria of folly and fanaticism.

Now the men of thought, of cultivation, of reason, in the community ought to be an antidote to these dangerous influences. Having been instructed in the lessons of history and science and philosophy they are bound to contribute their knowledge to the service of society. As a rule they are willing enough to do this for pay, in the professions of law and medicine and teaching and divinity. What I plead for today is the wider, nobler, unpaid service which an educated man renders to society simply by being thoughtful and by helping other men to think.

Think, in the second place, of the duty which men of moral principle owe to society in regard to the evils which corrupt and degrade it. Of the existence of these evils we need to be reminded again and again, just because we are comparatively clean and decent and upright people. Men who live an orderly life are in great danger of doing nothing else. We wrap our virtue up in little bags of respectability and keep it in the storehouse of a safe reputation. But if it is genuine virtue it is worthy of a better purpose than that. It is fit, nay, it is designed and demanded, to be used as salt, for the purifying of human life.

I. Supplementary information

1. Salt of the earth

According to OED (Oxford English Dictionary), "the salt of the earth" refers to the excellent of the earth; formerly, in trivial use, the powerful, aristocratic, or wealthy; now also applied to a person or persons of great worthiness, reliability, honesty, etc. According to Longman Dictionary of Contemporary English, this expression means someone who is ordinary but good and honest.

2. History of the use of salt

The habitual use of salt is intimately connected with the advance from nomadic to agricultural life, a step in civilization that profoundly influenced the rituals and cults of almost all ancient nations. The gods were worshiped as the givers of the kindly fruits of the earth, and salt was usually included in sacrificial offerings consisting wholly or partly of cereal elements. Such offerings were prevalent among the Greeks and Romans and among a number of the Semitic peoples.

Covenants were ordinarily made over a sacrificial meal, in which salt was a necessary element. The preservative qualities of salt made it a peculiarly fitting symbol of an enduring compact, sealing it with an obligation to fidelity. The word salt thus acquired connotations of high esteem and honour in ancient and modern languages. Examples include the Arab avowal "There is salt between us," the Hebrew expression "to eat the salt of the palace," and the modern Persian phrase *namak ḥarām*, "untrue to salt" (i.e., disloyal or ungrateful). In English the term "salt of the earth" describes a person held in high esteem. (Britannica)

II. Questions to think about as you read the text

1. Judging from the text, probably in what kind of cultural context is the author making this speech?
2. In offering his advice to the listeners, what assumptions is the speaker making about Christians?

III. Suggested essay topics

1. What it takes to be the salt of the earth.
2. Why and where "salt" is needed in this age?

IV. Further reading

Sermon on the Mount

The Sermon on the Mount refers to a biblical collection of religious teachings and ethical sayings of Jesus of Nazareth, as found in Matthew, chapters 5–7. The sermon was addressed to disciples and a large crowd of listeners to guide them in a life of discipline based on a new law of love, even to enemies, as opposed to the old law of retribution. In the Sermon on the Mount are found many of the most familiar Christian homilies and sayings, including the Beatitudes and the Lord's Prayer. Following are excerpts from the Gospel of Matthew of the New Testament.

5.1 Now when Jesus saw the crowds, he went up on a mountainside and sat down. His disciples came to him, and he began to teach them.

5.11 "Blessed are you when people insult you, persecute you and falsely say all kinds of evil against you because of me.

5.12 Rejoice and be glad, because great is your reward in heaven, for in the same way they persecuted the prophets who were before you.

5.13 "You are the salt of the earth. But if the salt loses its saltiness, how can it be made salty again? It is no longer good for anything, except to be thrown out and trampled underfoot.

5.14 "You are the light of the world. A town built on a hill cannot be hidden.

5.15 Neither do people light a lamp and put it under a bowl. Instead they put it on its stand, and it gives light to everyone in the house.

5.16 In the same way, let your light shine before others, that they may see your good deeds and glorify your Father in heaven.

5.38 "You have heard that it was said, 'Eye for eye, and tooth for tooth.'

5.39 But I tell you, do not resist an evil person. If anyone slaps you on the right cheek, turn to them the other cheek also.

5.40 And if anyone wants to sue you and take your shirt, hand over your coat as well.

5.41 If anyone forces you to go one mile, go with them two miles.

5.42 Give to the one who asks you, and do not turn away from the one who wants to borrow from you.

5.43 "You have heard that it was said, 'Love your neighbor and hate your enemy.'

5.44 But I tell you, love your enemies and pray for those who persecute you,

5.45 that you may be children of your Father in heaven. He causes his sun to rise on the evil and the good, and sends rain on the righteous and the unrighteous.

5.46 If you love those who love you, what reward will you get? Are not even the tax collectors doing that?

5.47 And if you greet only your own people, what are you doing more than others? Do not even pagans do that?

5.48 Be perfect, therefore, as your heavenly Father is perfect.

Progress[1]

"THOUGHT," says Pascal,[2] "makes the greatness of man." The universe can destroy an individual by a mere breath; but even if the entire force of the universe, were employed to destroy a single man, the man "would still be more noble than that which destroys him, since he is aware of his own death and of the advantage which the universe has over him: of all this the universe knows nothing." This awareness of himself and of the universe is no doubt what chiefly distinguishes man from all other forms of life. Man alone is conscious in the sense that he alone can stand outside of himself, as it were, and watch himself functioning for a brief span in the universe of which he is part. Man alone can coordinate memory of things past, perception of things present, anticipation of things to come, sufficiently so at least to know that he, like generations before him and after him, will live his brief span and will die. It is in virtue of

---

1 By Carl Becker, reprinted from *The Encyclopedia of the Social Sciences*, Vol XII, MacMillan, 1934.
2 Blaise Pascal (1623–1662), French philosopher, mathematician, and physicist, known for his writing about religion, and for his many important scientific discoveries. His major works are *Lettres écrites à un provincial* (1656), *Pensées de M. Pascal sur la religion et sur quelques autres sujets* (1670).

this awareness, and somewhat in proportion to its intensity, that man alone asks the fundamental questions. Why and for what purpose this brief and precarious existence in a universe that endures? What is man's relation to the universe that is sometimes friendly, sometimes hostile, but in the end always fatal to him? How may he elude its hostility, win its favor, find compensations for the intolerable certainty of the death which it will inflict upon him? The answers which men have given to these questions are to be found in the various myths, religious doctrines, philosophical and ethical interpretations which they have accepted, and in those unconsciously held preconceptions which in every age so largely shape their thought and conduct. The modern idea of progress belongs in this category of answers to necessary but insoluble questions. Like the myths of primitive peoples and the religious and philosophical beliefs of more advanced societies, it springs from the nature of man as a conscious creature, who finds existence intolerable unless he can enlarge and enrich his otherwise futile activities by relating them to something more enduring and significant than himself.

Although grounded in the nature of man as a conscious creature, the idea of progress belongs historically to the European tradition, and its origin may be derived from two sources. One of these is the classical conception of history as an endless series of cycles; the other is the Hebraic-Christian doctrine of messianic intervention and salvation. In Greek mythology the reign of Cronus (or Cronos) was regarded as a golden age when men lived like gods free from toil and grief. The present appeared to be a period of degeneration, and improvement or progress could be conceived only in terms of regeneration — a return to the lost golden age. After the myth ceased to be believed, the Greeks continued to look back to the time of great lawgivers, such as Lycurgus and Solon,[1] whose

---

1 Lycurgus, 9th-century BCE Spartan lawgiver; Solon (c. 630–c. 560 BCE), Athenian lawgiver and one of the Seven Wise Men of Greece.

work they idealized, and forward to the time when other great lawgivers would appear and give them better laws again. "Until philosophers become kings ...," said Plato, "cities will not cease from ill." Yet however often restoration was accomplished by inspired lawgivers or philosopher-kings, fate and human frailty would again bring degeneration; so that, since "time is the enemy of man," most classical writers regarded human history as an endless series of cycles, a continual repetition of the familiar phenomena of recovery and degeneration. The rational mind, according to Marcus Aurelius,[1] "stretches forth into the infinitude of Time, and comprehends the cyclical Regeneration of all things, and ... discerns that our children will see nothing fresh, just as our fathers too never saw anything more than we."[2] To regenerate the Roman Empire was obviously less easy than to construct a constitution for a small city-state; and Marcus Aurelius, philosopher-king though he was, instead of giving new laws to society recommended that the individual cultivate resignation. The later centuries of the Roman Empire, when resignation became at once more necessary and more difficult, were therefore a suitable time for the hopeless classical doctrine of endless cycles to be replaced by the Hebraic-Christian doctrine of messianic intervention and salvation.

The Jews like the Greeks looked back to a golden age, but it was identified with the creation of the world and with the Garden of Eden, in which the first men lived in innocence. Like the Greeks the Jews regarded the present as a period of degeneration, but they attributed the "fall" to Adam's disobedience to God's commands. God was at once the omniscient creator of the world and the supreme lawgiver, so that

---

1 Marcus Aurelius, Roman emperor (121–180), best known for his *Meditations* on Stoic philosophy. Marcus Aurelius has symbolized for many generations in the West the Golden Age of the Roman Empire.
2 *The Communings with Himself of Marcus Aurelius Antonillus*, tr. by C. R. Haines, Loeb Classical Library, London 1916, bk. XI, sect. I.

regeneration was identified with the coming of a God-inspired king of the house of David.[1] Multiplied reverses and the destruction of the Hebraic state gave to this doctrine a less political, a more mystical and transcendent character. The once actual but now vanished kingdom was replaced by an ideal Israel, symbolized as the "son of man;"[2] and the idea of a God-inspired king was replaced by the idea of a Messiah who would effect a catastrophic intervention in the affairs of men and pronounce a doomlike judgment on the world. The Christian myth was but an elaboration of these ideas. Jesus, son of man, son of God, was the Messiah. But the end was not yet. The death of Jesus was expiation for the sins of men, faith in Him the means of salvation. Jesus the man was dead, but Christ[3] the Lord still lived and would come again; then the earthly city would be destroyed and all the faithful be gathered with God in the heavenly city, there to dwell in perfection forever.

The weakness of the classical version of degeneration and recovery was that it offered no ultimate hope; of the Jewish, that its promise was for the chosen people only. The strength of the Christian version was that, conceiving human history as a cosmic drama in which all men played their predestined part, it offered to all the hope of eternal life as a compensation for the frustrations of temporal existence: by transferring the golden age from the past to the future it substituted an optimistic for a disillusioned view of human destiny. It is easily to be understood that such a view won wide assent in the Roman Empire during the centuries

---

1 King David (?–c. 962 BCE), in the Old Testament of the Bible, one of the Kings of Israel.
2 Often capitalized, God's divine representative destined to preside over the final judgment of the world.
3 The Messiah or "Lord's Anointed" whose advent was the subject of Jewish prophecy and expectation. It is also the title given to Jesus of Nazareth, as embodying the fulfilment of Messianic prophecy and expectation. Since the earliest Christian times it has been treated as a proper name.

(300–500) of declining prosperity and increasing oppression or that it served so well to make existence tolerable in the relatively anarchic, isolated and static society of western Europe from the dissolution of the Roman Empire to the Renaissance of classical learning. But it lost its hold on the imaginations of men as a result of profound changes in the outward conditions of life which occurred in western Europe from the fourteenth to the nineteenth century. Among these changes were the rise of ordered secular governments, the growth of towns and industry, the geographical discoveries and the extension of commerce which brought western Europe into direct contact with alien customs and ideas, and above all the rise of an educated middle class whose interests were hampered by a form of society in which both the power and the doctrines of the Christian church supported the autocracy of kings and the privileges of a landed aristocracy. It was in this time of revolt against ecclesiastical and secular authority that the Christian doctrine of salvation was gradually transformed into the modern idea of progress.

So long as Christian philosophy was little questioned, men could afford to ignore the factual experience of mankind since they were so well assured of its ultimate significance. But the declining influence of the church was accompanied by an increasing interest in the worldly activities of men in the past. Italian humanists turned to the study of classical writers; Protestant reformers appealed from current theologians to the beliefs and practises of the primitive church. Thus was born the modern historical approach to problems, and human life came increasingly to be regarded rather as a historical process than as a finished drama to be played out according to a divine plan. Seen in historical perspective, classical civilization emerged for the humanists as a resplendent epoch from which the middle period of ecclesiastical ascendancy[1] was

---

1 Commonly referred to as the Middle Ages.

manifestly a degeneration. Until the seventeenth century secular thought and learning turned for inspiration to the past — to the golden ages of Pericles[1] and Augustus;[2] and classical writers were idealized as models to be imitated, to be equaled if possible but hardly to be surpassed. In all this there was nothing that could not be found in the Greek notion of history with its cycles of recovery and degeneration, and but for two general influences modern thought might have been no more than a return to the classical view of human destiny.

One of these influences was Christian philosophy itself. Although it was gradually discredited as an account of events historically verifiable, Christian philosophy had so thoroughly habituated men to the thought of an ultimate happy destiny that they could never be content with a pale imitation of Greek pessimism. The other influence was experimental science which, in proportion as it displaced the Christian notion of a utopian existence after death to be brought about by the miraculous intervention of God, opened up the engaging prospect of indefinite improvement in this life to be effected by the application of human reason to the mastery of the physical and social environment which determines men's lives for good or ill.

In the seventeenth century Galileo and Newton made possible a new attitude toward nature. Nature was now seen to be friendly to man since the universe behaved in a uniform way according to universal natural laws — a behavior capable of being observed and measured and

---

1 Pericles (495–429BCE), Athenian statesman largely responsible for the full development, in the later 5th century BCE, of both the Athenian democracy and the Athenian empire, making Athens the political and cultural focus of Greece. His achievements included the construction of the Acropolis, begun in 447 BCE.

2 Also called Augustus Caesar or (until 27 BCE) Octavian (63 BCE–14 CE), first Roman emperor, following the republic, which had been finally destroyed by the dictatorship of Julius Caesar, his great-uncle and adoptive father. He overhauled every aspect of Roman life and brought durable peace and prosperity to the Greco-Roman world.

subjected to the uses of men. God was still the supreme lawgiver, the author of the universe; but His will was revealed in the great book of nature which men were to study in order to interpret, and to interpret in order that their ideas and customs might attain an increasing perfection by being brought into greater harmony with the laws of nature and of nature's God. God's revelation to men was thus made not through an inspired book or a divinely established church but through His works, and man had been endowed with reason precisely that he might learn through the course of the centuries what that revelation was. It was therefore no longer so necessary to think of the golden age of Greece and Rome as unsurpassable. "Those whom we call the ancients were really those who lived in the youth of the world," said Pascal, and "as we have added the experience of the ages between us and them to what they knew, it is in ourselves that is to be found that antiquity which we venerate in others." In the ascription of antiquity to the race there is still the implication of degeneration; but if a continuously richer experience made the moderns wiser than the ancients, it was not difficult to hit upon the idea that future generations would, in virtue of the same advantages, surpass the moderns. "We have admired our ancestors less," said Chastellux, "but we have loved our contemporaries better, and have expected more of our descendants." [1] Thus in the eighteenth century the modern idea of progress was born. Under the pressure of social discontents the dream of perfection, that necessary compensation for the limitations of the present state, having long been identified with the golden age or the Garden of Eden or life eternal in the heavenly city of God, was at last projected into the temporal life of man on earth and identified with the desired and hoped for regeneration of society.

---

1 *De la félicité publique*, 2 vols., new ed. Paris 1822, vol. ii, p. 71.

As formulated by the *philosophes*[1] the doctrine of progress was but a modification, however important, of the Christian doctrine of redemption; what was new in it was faith in the goodness of man and the efficacy of conscious reason to create an earthly utopia. The French Revolution was the outward expression of this faith. In the nineteenth century the doctrine of progress still reigned and won even a wider popular support, but it was somewhat differently conceived. After the disillusionment occasioned by the revolution and the Napoleonic conquests the prevailing desire was for social stability and national independence. The rationalization of this desire was provided by the historians and jurists who formulated the notion of historical continuity and deprecated the attempt to transform institutions according to a rational plan. Change was considered necessary but was thought to be beneficial only when it issued spontaneously from national tradition; the concept of natural law was not abandoned, but it was regarded as implicit in historical evolution rather than as a conclusion from abstract reason. Law is not made by the legislator, said Savigny,[2] any more than language is made by the grammarian. Ranke,[3] who influenced three generations of historians, viewed progress as something to be discovered by tracing the history of each nation just as it had occurred and by noting the peculiar contribution which each nation at the appropriate moment had made to European civilization. Hegel formulated the point of view of early nineteenth century jurists and historians in his *Philosophie der Geschichte* (Philosophy of History). A reason of nature working over the heads of men, a transcendent *Vernunft*

---

1 French for intellectuals, specifically those active during the Enlightenment of the 18th century.
2 Friedrich Karl von Savigny (1779–1861), German jurist and legal scholar who was one of the founders of the influential "historical school" of jurisprudence.
3 Leopold von Ranke (1795–1886), leading German historian of the 19th century, whose scholarly method and way of teaching (he was the first to establish a historical seminar) had a great influence on Western historiography.

(reason) reconciling within its cloudy recesses innumerable and conflicting *Verstände* (understanding), progressively realized itself in the actual events of history.

After the middle of the century natural science invested the doctrine of progress with a more materialistic implication. Progress was still regarded as the result of a force external to man; but the force was to be found not above but inherent in the phenomenal world. This view found support in the Darwinian theory of struggle for existence and survival of the fittest and in Schopenhauer's[1] doctrine of the will as an aspect of a universal blind force. Guided by these preconceptions thinkers abandoned the effort to hasten progress by describing utopias and turned to the search for the inevitable law by which progress had been and would be achieved. Of the many efforts of this sort the most important were those of Auguste Comte[2] and Karl Marx. Comte looked upon history as the result of the instinctive effort of men to ameliorate their condition — an effort which could be observed to fall into three stages of culture, the theological, the metaphysical and the positive, or scientific. Marx, interpreting the historic process in terms of Hegel's[3] famous dialectic, found the determining force in the economic class conflict which, having substituted the nineteenth century capitalist competitive society for the aristocratic landed society of the Middle Ages

---

1 Arthur Schopenhauer (1788–1860), German philosopher, often called the "philosopher of pessimism," who was primarily important as the exponent of a metaphysical doctrine of the will in immediate reaction against Hegelian idealism. His most important work is *The World as Will and Representation* (1818).

2 Comte (1798–1857), French philosopher known as the founder of sociology and of Positivism. Comte gave the science of sociology its name and established the new subject in a systematic fashion. His ideas are presented in *Cours de philosophie positive* (1830–1842; tr. *The Course of Positive Philosophy,* 1896 ed.), *Le Système de politique positive* (1851–1854; tr. *System of Positive Polity,* 1875–1877) and *Catechisme positiviste* (1852, tr. 1858) and *Synthèse subjective* (1856).

3 W. F. Hegel (1770–1831), German philosopher who had great influence on European and US philosophy with books such as *The Phenomenology of the Mind*.

and early modern times, would in turn replace the capitalist competitive society of the nineteenth century by the proletarian communist society of the future.

Of the many theories of progress formulated in the nineteenth century the only one that had much influence on the thought of common men was that of Marx. Yet the idea of progress, vaguely conceived as a rapid movement in general prosperity and happiness, became a living force. The chief reason for this was no doubt the rapid changes in the outward conditions of life consequent upon the technological revolution. The common man, before whose eyes the marvels of science and invention were constantly displayed, noted the unprecedented increase in wealth, the growth of cities, the new and improved methods of transportation and communication, the greater security from disease and death and all the conveniences of domestic life unknown to previous generations, and accepted the doctrine of progress without question: the world was obviously better than it had been, obviously would be better than it was. The precise objective toward which the world was progressing remained, however, for the common man and for the intellectual, somewhat vague.

Thus the nineteenth century doctrine of progress differed somewhat from that of the eighteenth. The difference may be expressed, with some exaggeration in the contrast, by saying that whereas the eighteenth century held that man can by taking thought add a cubit to his stature, the nineteenth century held that a cubit would be added to his stature whether he took thought or not. This latter faith that the stars were carrying men on to better things received a rude shock during the World War and subsequently; and there may be noted two significant changes in the present attitude toward the doctrine of progress. Certain thinkers, notably Spengler, are returning to the Greek notion of cycles, now formulated in terms of the rise, flourishing and decline of "cultures." Others are reverting to the eighteenth century idea that by deliberate purpose and the rational use of knowledge man can reconstruct society according to a more just and intelligible design. To this class belong those who have faith in communism, fascism and the planned capitalist society.

The doctrine of progress is peculiarly suited to western society in modern times; that is, a highly dynamic society capable of seeing its achievements against a long historical background. From the practical and from the rational point of view there is no reason to suppose that it will have a more enduring virtue than other doctrines which it has supplanted. If, as may well happen, the possibilities of scientific discovery and of technological invention should sometime be exhausted, the outward conditions of life might become sufficiently stabilized so that the idea of progress would cease to be relevant. Rationally considered, the idea of progress is always at war with its premises. It rests upon the notion of a universe in perpetual flux; yet the idea of progress has always carried the implication of finality, for it seems to be meaningless unless there is movement toward some ultimate objective. The formal theories of progress are all vitiated by this radical inconsistency. In Hegel's scheme the objective was freedom, already realized in the Prussian state. In Comte's theory the objective was the final positive stage into which Europe had already entered. Marx criticized Hegel for explaining history by a process which would not explain the future, but he is himself open to the criticism of having explained history in terms of a class conflict which would end with the establishment of a classless society. It is easy to picture history as a process working toward an ultimate good if the world is to come to an end when that good is attained; but if the universe as presented by modern science is to be accepted — a universe in perpetual flux — then a law of history which at some determinate time ceases to apply leaves much to be desired.

Thus the final good, absolute standards of value are sought in vain; there is merely a universe in which the ideas of things as well as the things themselves arise out of temporary conditions and are transformed with the modification of the conditions out of which they arose. On this assumption we must dispense with the notion of finality, must suppose that the idea of progress and all of its special formulations are but temporary insights useful for the brief moment in which they flourish. "In escaping from the illusion of finality, is it legitimate to exempt that dogma itself? Must not it, too, submit to its own negation of finality? Will not that process of change, for which Progress is the optimistic name, compel 'Progress' too to fall from the commanding position in which it is now, with apparent security, enthroned?"[1] The price we pay for escaping from the illusion of finality is the recognition that nothing, not even the belief that we have escaped that illusion, is likely to endure. All philosophies based upon the absolute and the unconditioned have their defects; but all philosophies based upon the universal relativity of things have their defects also, a minor one being that they must be prepared, at the appropriate moment, to commit *hara-kiri*[2] in deference to the ceaseless change which they postulate.

Belief in progress as a fact depends upon the standard of value chosen for measuring it and upon the time perspective in which it is measured. If we look back a hundred years, it is obvious that there has been progress in the mastery of physical forces. If we look back two thousand years, it is uncertain whether there has been much if any progress in intelligence and the art of living. If we look back two hundred and fifty thousand years, it is apparent that there has been progress in all those aspects of life which civilized men regard as valuable. All these judgments are based on standards of value appreciable by the mind of civilized man. But if we take a still longer perspective and estimate the universe as a whole, as an omniscient intelligence indifferent to human values might estimate it, in terms of

---

1 Bury, J. B., *The Idea of Progress*, p. 352.
2 Japanese, meaning "cutting the belly."

cosmic energy, then progress and the very existence of man himself become negligible and meaningless. In such a perspective we should see the whole life of man on the earth as a mere momentary ripple on the surface of one of the minor planets in one of the minor stellar systems.

I. Supplementary information

1. King David

David is believed to have written some of the Psalms. His friendship with Jonathan is thought of as an example of a perfect, loyal friendship between two people. When David was a boy, he killed the giant Goliath by hitting him on the head with a stone thrown from his sling. People sometimes use the names David and Goliath to describe a situation in which a small and less powerful person or group is fighting a much larger and more powerful person or group. (Britannica)

2. Dialectic

Originally used to refer to the nature of logical argument, but in the 19th century this term underwent something of a revaluation, and came to be associated with the work of the German philosophers Kant and Hegel. "Dialectic" referred to the process whereby the "idea" (*thesis*) was self-divided, and its internal oppositions (*antithesis*) were resolved in a synthesis which opened the way to a higher truth. In Marxist thinking "dialectic" refers to the contradictions present in any one phenomenon, and to their resolution through conflict. It is the nature of that opposition and that conflict which determines movement and change. (*Prentice Hall Guide to English Literature*)

3. Hegel's Philosophy of History

    Hegel regards history as an intelligible process moving towards a specific condition — the realization of human freedom. Hegel incorporates a deeper historicism into his philosophical theories than his predecessors or successors. He regards the relationship between "objective" history and the subjective development of the individual consciousness ("spirit") as an intimate one; this is a central thesis in his *Phenomenology of Spirit* (1807). And he views it to be a central task for philosophy to comprehend its place in the unfolding of history. Hegel constructs world history into a narrative of stages of human freedom, from the public freedom of the polis and the citizenship of the Roman Republic, to the individual freedom of the Protestant Reformation, to the civic freedom of the modern state. He attempts to incorporate the civilizations of India and China into his understanding of world history, though he regards those civilizations as static and therefore pre-historical. (Stanford Encyclopedia)

II. Questions to think about as you read the text

1. What seems to be the main purpose of this article?
2. Why does the author begin by comparing the power of the universe with individual human being?
3. What attitude towards progress on the part of the author can be inferred from his discussion on the seeming contradiction within the notion of progress itself?

III. Suggested essay topics

1. Discuss the concept of progress from a perspective not covered by the author.
2. Progress is a perception.

IV. Further reading

1. The Victorian Notion of Progress

   Richard D. Altick in his *Victorian People and Ideas* (Norton, 1973) discusses the Victorians' perception of time, their belief in progress, and the complexities and criticisms associated with it. According to Altick, the Victorians saw time and change as inseparable, and they lived in a period of significant change. They believed in moving forward and saw change as progress, even if this belief was sometimes shallow and unsupported. The progress they observed stemmed from advancements in science and technology, enabling humans to conquer the physical environment and benefit from scientific knowledge. However, not all Victorians unquestioningly embraced the idea of progress. Some recognized the possibility of progress in one area being offset by regression in another. Authors like Charles Dickens and influential voices like Carlyle, Arnold, and Ruskin questioned the notion of progress and presented a gloomier view of society. The Victorian poets, unlike their Romantic predecessors, did not wholeheartedly celebrate progress. The central question that arose was whether these "improvements" and machinery brought true happiness and contentment, as the means became more important than the ends. The metaphor of machinery represented both technological and social innovations, but the value of these innovations lay in their purpose and outcome rather than in their existence alone.

2. Becker, Carl L. *The Heavenly City of the Eighteenth-century Philosophers*. 2nd ed. Yale University Press, 2003.

Of Sympathy[1]

How selfish soever man may be supposed, there are evidently some principles in his nature, which interest him in the fortune of others, and render their happiness necessary to him, though he derives nothing from it, except the pleasure of seeing it. Of this kind is pity or compassion, the emotion which we feel for the misery of others, when we either see it, or are made to conceive it in a very lively manner. That we often derive sorrow from the sorrow of others, is a matter of fact too obvious to require any instances to prove it; for this sentiment, like all the other original passions of human nature, is by no means confined to the virtuous and humane, though they perhaps may feel it with the most exquisite sensibility. The greatest ruffian, the most hardened violator of the laws of society, is not altogether without it.

As we have no immediate experience of what other men feel, we can form no idea of the manner in which they are affected, but by conceiving what we ourselves should feel in the like situation. Though our brother is upon the rack, as long as we ourselves are at our ease, our senses will never

---

1 Adam Smith, *The Theory of Moral Sentiments* (1759), Section I, "Of the Sense and Propriety," from Part I, "Of the Propriety of Action," with minor editing in punctuation and spelling.

inform us of what he suffers. They never did and never can carry us beyond our own person, and it is by the imagination only that we can form any conception of what are his sensations. Neither can that faculty help us to this any other way, than by representing to us what would be our own, if we were in his case. It is the impressions of our own senses only, not those of his, which our imaginations copy. By the imagination we place ourselves in his situation, we conceive ourselves enduring all the same torments, we enter as it were into his body and become in some measure him, and thence form some idea of his sensations and even feel something which, though weaker in degree, is not altogether unlike them. His agonies, when they are thus brought home to ourselves, when we have thus adopted and made them our own, begin at last to affect us, and we then tremble and shudder at the thought of what he feels. For as to be in pain or distress of any kind excites the most excessive sorrow, so to conceive or to imagine that we are in it, excites some degree of the same emotion, in proportion to the vivacity or dullness of the conception.

That this is the source of our fellow-feeling for the misery of others, that it is by changing places in fancy with the sufferer, that we come either to conceive or to be affected by what he feels, may be demonstrated by many obvious observations, if it should not be thought sufficiently evident of itself. When we see a stroke aimed and just ready to fall upon the leg or arm of another person, we naturally shrink and draw back our own leg or our own arm; and when it does fall, we feel it in some measure, and are hurt by it as well as the sufferer. The mob, when they are gazing at a dancer on the slack rope, naturally writhe and twist and balance their own bodies, as they see him do, and as they feel that they themselves must do if in his situation. Persons of delicate fibres and a weak constitution of body, complain that in looking on the sores and ulcers which are exposed by beggars in the streets, they are apt to feel an itching or uneasy sensation in the correspondent part of their own bodies. The horror which they conceive at the misery of those wretches affects that particular part in themselves more than any other; because that horror arises from conceiving what they themselves would suffer, if they really were the wretches whom they are looking upon, and if that particular part in themselves was actually affected in the same miserable manner. The very force of this conception is sufficient, in their feeble frames, to produce that itching or uneasy sensation complained of. Men of the most robust make, observe that in looking upon sore eyes they often feel a very sensible soreness in their own, which proceeds from the same reason; that organ being in the strongest man more delicate than any other part of the body is in the weakest.

Neither is it those circumstances only, which create pain or sorrow, that call forth our fellow-feeling. Whatever is the passion which arises from any object in the person principally concerned, an analogous emotion springs up, at the thought of his situation, in the breast of every attentive spectator. Our joy for the deliverance of those heroes of tragedy or romance who interest us, is as sincere as our grief for their distress, and our fellow-feeling with their misery is not more real than that with their happiness. We enter into their gratitude towards those faithful friends who did not desert them in their difficulties; and we heartily go along with their resentment against those perfidious traitors who injured, abandoned, or deceived them. In every passion of which the mind of man is susceptible, the emotions of the by-stander always correspond to what, by bringing the case home to himself, he imagines, should be the sentiments of the sufferer.

Pity and compassion are words appropriated to signify our fellow-feeling with the sorrow of others. Sympathy, though its meaning was, perhaps, originally the same, may now, however, without much impropriety, be made use of to denote our fellow-feeling with any passion whatever.

Upon some occasions sympathy may seem to arise merely from the view of a certain emotion in another person. The passions, upon some occasions, may seem to be transfused from one man to another, instantaneously, and antecedent to any knowledge of what excited them in the person principally concerned. Grief and joy, for example, strongly expressed in the look and gestures of any one, at once affect the spectator with some degree of a like painful or agreeable emotion. A smiling face is, to everybody that sees it, a cheerful object; as a sorrowful countenance, on the other hand, is a melancholy one.

This, however, does not hold universally, or with regard to every passion. There are some passions of which the expressions excite no sort of sympathy, but before we are acquainted with what gave occasion to them, serve rather to disgust and provoke us against them. The furious behavior of an angry man is more likely to exasperate us against himself than against his enemies. As we are unacquainted with his provocation, we cannot bring his case home to ourselves, nor conceive anything like the passions which it excites. But we plainly see what is the situation of those with whom he is angry, and to what violence they may be exposed from so enraged an adversary. We readily, therefore, sympathize with their fear or resentment, and are immediately disposed to take part against the man from whom they appear to be in so much danger.

If the very appearances of grief and joy inspire us with some degree of the like emotions, it is because they suggest to us the general idea of some good or bad fortune that has befallen the person in whom we observe them: and in these passions this is sufficient to have some little influence upon us. The effects of grief and joy terminate in the person who feels those emotions, of which the expressions do not, like those of resentment, suggest to us the idea of any other person for whom we are concerned, and whose interests are opposite to his. The general idea of good or bad fortune, therefore, creates some concern for the person who has met with it, but the general idea of provocation excites no sympathy with the anger of the man who has received it. Nature, it seems, teaches us to be more averse to enter[1] into this passion,

---

1   In contemporary usage, "averse to" is usually followed by a noun or the "-ing" form of a verb.

and, till informed of its cause, to be disposed rather to take part against it.

Even our sympathy with the grief or joy of another, before we are informed of the cause of either, is always extremely imperfect. General lamentations, which express nothing but the anguish of the sufferer, create rather a curiosity to inquire into his situation, along with some disposition to sympathize with him, than any actual sympathy that is very sensible. The first question which we ask is, What has befallen you? Till this be answered, though we are uneasy both from the vague idea of his misfortune, and still more from torturing ourselves with conjectures about what it may be, yet our fellow-feeling is not very considerable.

Sympathy, therefore, does not arise so much from the view of the passion, as from that of the situation which excites it. We sometimes feel for another, a passion of which he himself seems to be altogether incapable; because when we put ourselves in his case, that passion arises in our breast from the imagination, though it does not in his from the reality. We blush for the impudence and rudeness of another, though he himself appears to have no sense of the impropriety of his own behavior; because we cannot help feeling with what confusion we ourselves should be covered, had we behaved in so absurd a manner.

Of all the calamities to which the condition of mortality exposes mankind, the loss of reason appears, to those who have the least spark of humanity, by far the most dreadful, and they behold that last stage of human wretchedness with deeper commiseration than any other. But the poor wretch, who is in it, laughs and sings perhaps, and is altogether insensible of his own misery. The anguish which humanity feels, therefore, at the sight of such an object, cannot be the reflection of any sentiment of the sufferer. The compassion of the spectator must arise altogether from the consideration of what he himself would feel if he was reduced to the same unhappy situation, and, what perhaps is impossible, was at the same time able to regard it with his present reason and judgment.

What are the pangs of a mother when she hears the moanings of her infant that during the agony of disease cannot express what it feels? In her idea of what it suffers, she joins, to its real helplessness, her own consciousness of that helplessness, and her own terrors for the unknown consequences of its disorder; and out of all these, forms, for her own sorrow, the most complete image of misery and distress. The infant, however, feels only the uneasiness of the present instant, which can never be great. With regard to the future, it is perfectly secure, and in its thoughtlessness and want of foresight, possesses an antidote against fear and anxiety, the great tormentors of the human breast, from which reason and philosophy will in vain attempt to defend it, when it grows up to a man.

We sympathize even with the dead, and overlooking what is of real importance in their situation, that awful futurity which awaits them, we are chiefly affected by those circumstances which strike our senses, but can have no influence upon their happiness. It is miserable, we think, to be deprived of the light of the sun; to be shut out from life and conversation; to be laid in the cold grave, a prey to corruption and the reptiles of the earth; to be no more thought of in this world, but to be obliterated in a little time from the affections and almost from the memory of their dearest friends and relations. Surely, we imagine, we can never feel too much for those who have suffered so dreadful a calamity. The tribute of our fellow-feeling seems doubly due to them now, when they are in danger of being forgot by everybody; and, by the vain honors which we pay to their memory, we endeavor, for our own misery, artificially to keep alive our melancholy remembrance of their misfortune. That our sympathy can afford them no consolation seems to be an addition to their calamity; and to think that all we can do is unavailing, and that, what alleviates all other distress, the regret, the love, and the lamentations of their friends, can yield no comfort to them, serves only to exasperate our sense of their misery. The happiness of the dead, however, most assuredly, is affected by none of these circumstances; nor is it the thought of these things which can ever disturb the profound security of their repose. The idea of that dreary and endless melancholy, which the fancy naturally ascribes to their condition, arises altogether from our joining to the change which has been produced upon them, our own consciousness of that change, from our putting ourselves in their situation, and from our lodging, if I may be allowed to say so, our own living souls in their inanimated bodies, and thence conceiving what would be our emotions in this case. It is from this very illusion of the imagination, that the foresight of our own dissolution is so terrible to us, and that the idea of those circumstances, which undoubtedly can give us no pain when we are dead, makes us miserable while we are alive. And from thence arises one of the most important principles in human nature, the dread of death, the great poison to the happiness, but the great restraint upon the injustice of mankind, which, while it afflicts and mortifies the individual, guards and protects the society.

I. Supplementary information

Adam Smith

Adam Smith (1723–1790) was a Scottish economist, philosopher, and author who is widely regarded as the father of modern economics. Born in Kirkcaldy, Scotland, Smith's groundbreaking ideas and influential writings laid the foundation for classical economics and continue to shape economic theory to this day. His most renowned work, *The Wealth of Nations*, published in 1776, established him as a key figure in the Scottish Enlightenment and revolutionized the understanding of free markets, division of labor, and the role of self-interest in economic systems. Smith's ideas emphasized the power of competition, specialization, and the invisible hand of the market as drivers of economic growth and prosperity. His profound insights into the nature of markets and human behaviour have had a lasting impact on the fields of economics, political science, and philosophy, cementing his place as one of history's most influential thinkers.

His earlier work, *The Theory of Moral Sentiments*, delves into the realm of moral philosophy. In this seminal book, Smith examines how individuals develop a sense of morality and how moral judgments are influenced by our capacity for empathy and sympathy for others. While often overshadowed by Smith's later work on economics, this book remains an essential text for those interested in the intersection of ethics, philosophy, and human nature.

II. Questions to think about as you read the text

1. In what way does Smith's book on moral sentiments reflect the cultural and historical background of his age?
2. What relationship between sympathy and social order can be inferred from Adam Smith's discussion on moral sentiments?

III. Suggested essay topics

1. Write an essay on the moral value of imagination. Illustrate your point with your own experiences.
2. Write an essay on the power of sentiments in our everyday life. Base your discussion on real-life examples.

IV. Further reading

Following is an excerpt from Smith's Wealth of Nations. This and Moral Sentiments, though treating of seemingly very different subject matters, are both typical of the age that produced them. They are studies on human society and individuals from an approach that is secular, empiricist and rational.

From *Wealth of Nations*[1]

This division of labour, from which so many advantages are derived, is not originally the effect of any human wisdom, which foresees and intends that general opulence to which it gives occasion. It is the necessary, though very slow and gradual consequence of a certain propensity in human nature which has in view no such extensive utility; the propensity to truck, barter, and exchange one thing for another.

Whether this propensity be one of those original principles in human nature of which no further account can be given; or whether, as seems more probable, it be the necessary consequence of the faculties of reason and speech, it belongs not to our present subject to inquire. It is common to all men, and to be found in no other race of animals, which seem to know neither this nor any other species of contracts. Two greyhounds, in running down the same hare, have sometimes the appearance of acting in some sort of concert. Each turns her towards his companion, or endeavours to intercept her when his companion turns her towards himself. This, however, is not the effect of any contract, but of the accidental concurrence of their passions in the same object at that particular time. Nobody ever saw a dog make a fair and deliberate exchange of one bone for another with another dog. Nobody ever saw one animal by its gestures and natural cries signify to another, this is mine, that yours; I am willing to give this for that. When an animal wants to obtain something either of a man or of another animal, it has no other means of persuasion but to gain the favour of those whose service it requires. A puppy fawns upon its dam, and a spaniel endeavours by a thousand attractions to engage the attention of its master who is at dinner, when it wants to be fed by him. Man sometimes uses the same arts with his brethren,

---

1 Chapter II, Of the Principle which Gives Occasion to the Division of Labour.

and when he has no other means of engaging them to act according to his inclinations, endeavours by every servile and fawning attention to obtain their good will. He has not time, however, to do this upon every occasion. In civilised society he stands at all times in need of the co-operation and assistance of great multitudes, while his whole life is scarce sufficient to gain the friendship of a few persons.

In almost every other race of animals each individual, when it is grown up to maturity, is entirely independent, and in its natural state has occasion for the assistance of no other living creature. But man has almost constant occasion for the help of his brethren, and it is in vain for him to expect it from their benevolence only. He will be more likely to prevail if he can interest their self-love in his favour, and show them that it is for their own advantage to do for him what he requires of them. Whoever offers to another a bargain of any kind, proposes to do this. Give me that which I want, and you shall have this which you want, is the meaning of every such offer; and it is in this manner that we obtain from one another the far greater part of those good offices which we stand in need of. It is not from the benevolence of the butcher, the brewer, or the baker that we expect our dinner, but from their regard to their own interest. We address ourselves, not to their humanity but to their self-love, and never talk to them of our own necessities but of their advantages. Nobody but a beggar chooses to depend chiefly upon the benevolence of his fellow-citizens. Even a beggar does not depend upon it entirely. The charity of well-disposed people, indeed, supplies him with the whole fund of his subsistence. But though this principle ultimately provides him with all the necessaries of life which he has occasion for, it neither does nor can provide him with them as he has occasion for them. The greater part of his occasional wants are supplied in the same manner as those of other people, by treaty, by barter, and by purchase. With the money which one man gives him he purchases food. The old clothes which another bestows upon him he exchanges for other old clothes which suit him better, or for lodging, or for food, or for money, with which he can buy either food, clothes, or lodging, as he has occasion.

As it is by treaty, by barter, and by purchase that we obtain from one another the greater part of those mutual good offices which we stand in need of, so it is this same trucking disposition which originally gives occasion to the division of labour. In a tribe of hunters or shepherds a particular person makes bows and arrows, for example, with more readiness and dexterity than any other. He frequently exchanges them for cattle or for venison with his companions; and he finds at last that he can in this manner get more cattle and venison than if he himself went to the field to catch them. From a regard to his own interest, therefore, the making of bows and arrows grows to be his chief business, and he becomes a sort of armourer. Another excels in making the frames and covers of their little huts or movable houses. He is accustomed to be of use in this way to his neighbours, who reward him in the same manner with cattle and with venison, till at last he finds it his interest to dedicate himself entirely to this employment, and to become a sort of house-carpenter. In the same manner a third becomes a smith or a brazier, a fourth a tanner or dresser of hides or skins, the principal part of the nothing of savages. And thus the certainty of being able to exchange all that surplus part of the produce of his own labour, which is over and above his own consumption, for such parts of the produce of other men's labour as he may have occasion for, encourages every man to apply himself to a particular occupation, and to cultivate and bring to perfection whatever talent or genius he may possess for that particular species of business.

The difference of natural talents in different men is, in reality, much less than we are aware of; and the very different genius which appears to distinguish men of different professions, when grown up to maturity, is not upon many occasions so much the cause as the effect of the division of labour. The difference between the most dissimilar characters, between a philosopher and a common street porter, for example, seems to arise not so much from nature as from habit, custom, and education. When they came into the world, and for the first six or eight years of their existence, they were perhaps very much alike, and neither their parents nor playfellows could perceive any remarkable difference. About that age, or soon after, they come to be employed in very different occupations. The difference of talents comes then to be taken notice of, and widens by degrees, till at last the vanity of the philosopher is willing to acknowledge scarce any resemblance. But without the disposition to truck, barter, and exchange, every man must have procured to himself every necessary and conveniency of life which he wanted. All must have had the same duties to perform, and the same work to do, and there could have been no such difference of employment as could alone give occasion to any great difference of talents.

As it is this disposition which forms that difference of talents, so remarkable among men of different professions, so it is this same disposition which renders that difference useful. Many tribes of animals acknowledged to be all of the same species derive from nature a much more remarkable distinction of genius, than what, antecedent to custom and education, appears to take place among men.

By nature a philosopher is not in genius and disposition half so different from a street porter, as a mastiff is from a greyhound, or a greyhound from a spaniel, or this last from a shepherd's dog. Those different tribes of animals, however, though all of the same species, are of scarce any use to one another. The strength of the mastiff is not, in the least, supported either by the swiftness of the greyhound, or by the sagacity of the spaniel, or by the docility of the shepherd's dog. The effects of those different geniuses and talents, for want of the power or disposition to barter and exchange, cannot be brought into a common stock, and do not in the least contribute to the better accommodation and conveniency of the species. Each animal is still obliged to support and defend itself, separately and independently, and derives no sort of advantage from that variety of talents with which nature has distinguished its fellows. Among men, on the contrary, the most dissimilar geniuses are of use to one another; the different produces of their respective talents, by the general disposition to truck, barter, and exchange, being brought, as it were, into a common stock, where every man may purchase whatever part of the produce of other men's talents he has occasion for.

Civilization and Culture[1]

Society has an inner environment which it makes, besides the outer which it only moulds. The former consists in the whole apparatus of custom and institution, the complex and multiform mechanism of order, the devices and instruments by which nature is controlled, the modes of expression and communication, the comforts, refinements, and luxuries which determine standards of living, and the economic system through which they are produced and distributed. It includes all that human intelligence and art have wrought to make the world a home for the human spirit. It includes alike the technological and the institutional equipment, parliaments and telephone exchanges, corporation charters and railroads, insurance agencies and automobiles. This whole apparatus of life we shall here call civilization. It is obvious that the political system belongs to this region and constitutes one great division of it.

From civilization we must distinguish culture as its animating and creating spirit. Civilization is the instrument, the body, even the garment of culture. Civilization expresses itself in politics, in economics, in technology, while culture expresses itself in art, in literature, in religion, in morals. Our

---

[1] Excerpted from *The Modern State* (1926) by R. M. MacIver.

culture is what we are, our civilization is what we use. There is a technique of culture, but the culture itself is not technique. Culture is the fulfilment of life, revealed in the things we want in themselves, and not in their results. No one wants banking systems and factories and ballot-boxes for any intrinsic significance they possess. If we could attain the products without the process we would gladly dispense with the latter. But the objects of culture have a direct significance. It is the difference between the mode of achieving and the thing achieved, between the way of living and the life led. The interest in technique is derivative, though like any other it may come to engross the mind, but the interest in culture is primary.

There is a great difference between an object of civilization and a work of culture. An institutional or technical achievement raises, so to speak, the level of civilization. It is an improvement on the past. Once the spinning machine or the railway-locomotive or the typewriter is discovered, men go on developing it. Civilization is cumulative. The new model betters the old, and renders it obsolete. The achievement perpetuates itself and is the basis of further achievement. Civilization is rightly described as a "march," for each step leads to another and is always forward. Great historical catastrophes can interrupt this cumulation, but nothing seems able to break it altogether. It is a poor age indeed that does not add some stones to this rising edifice of civilization. But culture is not cumulative. It has to be won afresh by each new generation. It is not a simple inheritance like civilization. It is true that here too past attainment is the basis of present achievement, but there is no surety that the present will equal, still less that it will improve on, the past. The heights reached by Greek art and Greek drama are not held by succeeding ages. The achievement of Dante or of Shakespeare is not equalled by those who follow them. What Archimedes or Galileo or Newton discovered is the basis of further discovery that exceeds any of theirs, but what Sophocles or Michael Angelo or Milton expressed is not expressed better or more fully by others who have their works before them. We do not deny that there is advance in culture also, but it is no steady advance. It is variable and seems capricious, subject to retreats and setbacks.

The reason thereof suggests another difference between civilization and culture. Culture must always be won afresh, because it is a direct expression of the human spirit. In a very real sense a musician composes only for musicians and an artist paints only for artists. A poet can write only for those who have themselves the poetic quality. Every work of art implies at least two artists, he who creates and he who understands, and so with all the achievements of culture. Cultural expression is communication between likes and is possible only by reason of their likeness. The work of the artist is only for other artists, but the work of the engineer is not for other engineers. The bridge-builder does not construct for other bridge-builders, but for those who themselves may appreciate nothing of his skill. Millions may use a technical invention without the least understanding of it. Devices for use are in fact the more perfect the less understanding they require, and the aim of the inventor is to make his invention, in the American phrase, "fool-proof." We would get an entirely false conception of the intelligence and capacity of our age, and an entirely false standard of comparison between it and other ages, if we judged it by its institutions and its technical equipment. Our estimate would be much more just if we judged it by the books men read and write, by the ideals they cherish, by the pleasures they pursue, by the religions which they practise, by all the things they really care about and think about.

It follows that one people can borrow civilization from another people in a way in which culture cannot be borrowed. Technical devices can be transplanted without change. Institutional devices, being more nearly related to the form of culture which they serve, undergo some change when they are borrowed. The barbarian can learn more easily to use the rifle than the ballot-box. The institutions of Western democracy do not accommodate themselves without strain to the social life of the Orient or even of South America. Nevertheless they are transferable to a degree, and have in fact been adopted in many countries to which they were not native. But a culture cannot be adopted. A culture may be assimilated gradually, by peoples who are ready for it and who are brought into constant contact with it, but even so they inevitably change it in making it their own. When extraneous considerations lead to the nominal acceptance of an alien culture it becomes a travesty or an empty form. The extraordinary transmogrifications of Christianity in the course of two thousand years, involving not merely the restatement but often the rejection of its original principles, offer a splendid illustration of the truth that a culture cannot be "adopted." The culture of a people expresses their character and can express nothing else. Hence civilization is far more pervasive than culture. Japan can speedily adopt the civilization of the West, but it neither can nor cares to adopt its culture. Of course we must not imply that the two factors are entirely separate. Civilization, whether native or adopted, is a kind of social environment, and human beings respond in similar ways to similar conditions. Civilization and culture necessarily react on one another. Nevertheless it seems clear that cultures can remain distinctive within the form of a common civilization. Given the means of communication, it is inevitable that civilization should become, in its larger aspects, one and universal. But under this seeming uniformity of life great cultural differences remain, both within and between the peoples of the earth.

One further distinction can now be made. We have pointed out that civilization, in contrast to culture, is cumulative. This is true in another sense also. Means can be massed into great engines of power. Systems can be extended into vaster systems. But culture resists the mechanics of addition and multiplication. I have elsewhere expressed this truth as follows:

"We can add the wealth of a group or a nation and get some kind of a total. We can add its man-power and get a total. But we cannot make a sum of its health or its habits or its culture. A thousand weak purposes cannot be rolled into one strong purpose as a thousand weak units of force are joined into one strong force. We cannot add wisdom as we can add wealth. A thousand mediocrities do not sum up into one genius."

I. Supplementary information

It is often argued that the concept of civilization is urban in origin while that of culture is agricultural. In the following passage, taken from The Story of Civilization *(with minor editing), Will Durant alludes to their different origins in his discussion on the conditions of civilization.*

Certain factors condition civilization, and may encourage or impede it. These include geographic conditions, economic conditions, etc ... Economic conditions are more important. A people may possess ordered institutions, a lofty moral code, and even a flair for the minor forms of art, like the American Indians; and yet if it remains in the hunting stage, if it depends for its existence upon the precarious fortunes of the chase, it will never quite pass from barbarism to civilization. A nomad stock, like the Bedouins of Arabia, may be exceptionally intelligent and vigorous, it may display high qualities of character like courage, generosity and nobility; but without that simple *sine qua non* of culture, a continuity of food, its intelligence will be lavished on the perils of the hunt and the tricks of trade, and nothing will remain for the laces and frills, the curtsies and amenities, the arts and comforts, of civilization. The first form of culture is agriculture. It is when man settles down to till the soil and lay up provisions for the uncertain future that he finds time and reason to be civilized. Within that little circle of security — a reliable supply of water and food — he builds his huts, his temples and his schools; he invents productive tools, and domesticates the dog, the ass, the pig, at last himself. He learns to work with regularity and order, maintains a longer tenure of life, and transmits more completely than before the mental and moral heritage of his race.

Culture suggests agriculture, but civilization suggests the city. In one aspect civilization is the habit of civility; and civility is the refinement which townsmen, who made the word, thought possible only in the *civitas* or city. For in the city are gathered, rightly or wrongly, the wealth and brains produced in the countryside; in the city invention and industry multiply comforts, luxuries and leisure; in the city traders meet, and barter goods and ideas; in that cross-fertilization of minds at the crossroads of trade intelligence is sharpened and stimulated to creative power. In the city some men are set aside from the making of material things, and produce science and philosophy, literature and art. Civilization begins in the peasant's hut, but it comes to flower only in the towns.

II. Questions to think about as you read the text

1. What is in culture that sets it apart from civilization and makes the former hard to "borrow"?
2. Try to find examples of civilization changing or producing an impact on culture.
3. In what way does this article corroborate "The Decline and Fall of Literature"?

III. Suggested essay topics

1. Cultural diversity in the midst of globalization.

2. What foreign holidays mean to us?

IV. Further reading

The following excerpt from Isaiah Berlin's The Roots of Romanticism, *explains the role of class difference between the French and German scholars in the rise of German romanticism. Interestingly, in Herder' criticism of the French scholars is implied the kind of difference between culture and civilization that our text discusses.*

The Roots of Romanticism

[Among the French scholars only] Diderot and Rousseau were commoners, real commoners. Diderot really did come from the poor. Rousseau was a Swiss, and therefore does not count in this category. Consequently, these persons spoke with a different language. They were no doubt oppositional, but they were oppositional against persons who came from the same class as themselves. They went to salons, they glittered, they were persons of high polish, great education, splendid prose style and a generous and handsome outlook on life.

Their mere existence irritated, humiliated and infuriated the Germans. When Herder came to Paris in the early 1770s, he was unable to get into contact with any of these men. It appeared to him that they were all artificial, highly mannered, extremely self conscious, dry, soulless little dancing-masters in salons who did not understand the inner life of man, who were debarred either by bad doctrine or by false origin from understanding the true purposes of men on earth and the true, rich, generous potentialities with which human beings had been endowed by God. This too helped to create a chasm between the Germans and the French — the mere thought of these *frondeurs*, the mere thought of this opposition, even on the part of those who themselves hated the Church of Rome, who themselves hated the King of

France, filled them with nausea, disgust, humiliation and inferiority, and this dug an enormous ditch between the Germans and the French which not even all the cultural interchanges which can be traced by scholars were able to overcome. This is perhaps one of the roots of the German opposition to the French from which romanticism began.

Federalist Papers, No. 10[1]

Among the numerous advantages promised by a well-constructed Union, none deserves to be more accurately developed than its tendency to break and control the violence of faction. The friend of popular governments never finds himself so much alarmed for their character and fate as when he contemplates their propensity to this dangerous vice. He will not fail, therefore, to set a due value on any plan which, without violating the principles to which he is attached, provides a proper cure for it. The instability, injustice, and confusion introduced into the public councils have, in truth, been the mortal diseases under which popular governments have everywhere perished, as they continue to be the favorite and fruitful topics from which the adversaries to liberty derive their most specious declamations. The valuable improvements made by the American constitutions on the popular models, both ancient and modern, cannot certainly be too much admired; but it would be an unwarrantable partiality to contend that they have as effectually obviated the danger on this side, as was wished and expected. Complaints are everywhere heard from our most considerate and virtuous

---

[1] Excerpted from *The Federalist Papers*, No. 10, by James Madison. This section discusses the causes and consequences of faction.

citizens, equally the friends of public and private faith and of public and personal liberty, that our governments are too unstable, that the public good is disregarded in the conflicts of rival parties, and that measures are too often decided, not according to the rules of justice and the rights of the minor party, but by the superior force of an interested and overbearing majority. However anxiously we may wish that these complaints had no foundation, the evidence of known facts will not permit us to deny that they are in some degree true. It will be found, indeed, on a candid review of our situation, that some of the distresses under which we labor have been erroneously charged on the operation of our governments; but it will be found, at the same time, that other causes will not alone account for many of our heaviest misfortunes; and, particularly, for that prevailing and increasing distrust of public engagements and alarm for private rights which are echoed from one end of the continent to the other. These must be chiefly, if not wholly, effects of the unsteadiness and injustice with which a factious spirit has tainted our public administration.

By a faction I understand a number of citizens, whether amounting to a majority or minority of the whole, who are united and actuated by some common impulse of passion, or of interest, adverse to the rights of other citizens, or to the permanent and aggregate interests of the community.

There are two methods of curing the mischiefs of faction: the one, by removing its causes; the other, by controlling its effects. There are again two methods of removing the causes of faction: the one, by destroying the liberty which is essential to its existence; the other, by giving to every citizen the same opinions, the same passions, and the same interests.

It could never be more truly said than of the first remedy that it was worse than the disease. Liberty is to faction what air is to fire, an aliment without which it instantly expires. But it could not be a less folly to abolish liberty, which is essential to political life, because it nourishes faction, than it would be to wish the annihilation of air, which is essential to animal life, because it imparts to fire its destructive agency.

The second expedient is as impracticable as the first would be unwise. As long as the reason of man continues fallible, and he is at liberty to exercise it, different opinions will be formed. As long as the connection subsists between his reason and his self-love, his opinions and his passions will have a reciprocal influence on each other; and the former will be objects to which the latter will attach themselves. The diversity in the faculties[1] of men, from which the rights of property originate, is not less an insuperable obstacle to a uniformity of interests. The protection of these faculties is the first object of government. From the protection of different and unequal faculties of acquiring property, the possession of different degrees and kinds of property immediately results; and from the influence of these on the sentiments and views of the respective proprietors ensues a division of the society into different interests and parties.

The latent causes of faction are thus sown in the nature of man; and we see them everywhere brought into different degrees of activity, according to the different circumstances of civil society. A zeal for different opinions concerning religion, concerning government, and many other points, as well of speculation as of practice; an attachment to different leaders ambitiously contending for pre-eminence and power; or to persons of other descriptions whose fortunes have been interesting to the human passions, have, in turn, divided mankind into parties, inflamed them with mutual animosity, and rendered them much more disposed to vex and oppress each other than to co-operate for their common good. So strong is this propensity of mankind to fall into mutual animosities that where no substantial occasion presents itself, the most frivolous and fanciful distinctions have been sufficient to kindle their unfriendly passions and excite their most violent conflicts. But the most common and durable source of factions has been the various and unequal

---

1 Pecuniary ability, means, resources; possessions, property (OED).

distribution of property. Those who hold and those who are without property have ever formed distinct interests in society. Those who are creditors, and those who are debtors, fall under a like discrimination. A landed interest, a manufacturing interest, a mercantile interest, a moneyed interest, with many lesser interests, grow up of necessity in civilized nations, and divide them into different classes, actuated by different sentiments and views. The regulation of these various and interfering interests forms the principal task of modern legislation and involves the spirit of party and faction in the necessary and ordinary operations of government.

No man is allowed to be a judge in his own cause, because his interest would certainly bias his judgment, and, not improbably, corrupt this integrity. With equal, nay with greater reason, a body of men are unfit to be both judges and parties at the same time; yet what are many of the most important acts of legislation but so many judicial determinations, not indeed concerning the rights of single persons, but concerning the rights of large bodies of citizens? And what are the different classes of legislators but advocates and parties to the causes which they determine? Is a law proposed concerning private debts? It is a question to which the creditors are parties on one side and the debtors on the other. Justice ought to hold the balance between them. Yet the parties are, and must be, themselves the judges; and the most numerous party, or in other words, the most powerful faction must be expected to prevail. Shall domestic manufacturers be encouraged, and in what degree, by restrictions on foreign manufacturers? are questions which would be differently decided by the landed and the manufacturing classes, and probably by neither with a sole regard to justice and the public good. The apportionment of taxes on the various descriptions of property is an act which seems to require the most exact impartiality; yet there is, perhaps, no legislative act in which greater opportunity and temptation are given to a predominant party to trample on the rules of justice. Every shilling with which they overburden the inferior number is a shilling saved to their own pockets.

It is in vain to say that enlightened statesmen will be able to adjust these clashing interests and render them all subservient to the public good. Enlightened statesmen will not always be at the helm. Nor, in many cases, can such an adjustment be made at all without taking into view indirect and remote considerations, which will rarely prevail over the immediate interest which one party may find in disregarding the rights of another or the good of the whole. The inference to which we are brought is that the *causes* of faction cannot be removed and that relief is only to be sought in the means of controlling its *effects*.

...

I. Supplementary information

The Federalist Papers

The Federalist Papers, a Series of 85 Political Essays, written 1787–88 under the pseudonym "Publius." Alexander Hamilton initiated the series with the immediate intention of persuading New York to approve the Federalist Constitution. He had as collaborators James Madison and John Jay. Hamilton certainly wrote 51 of the essays, Madison wrote 14, Jay 5; the authorship of 15 is in dispute (as between Hamilton and Madison). The essays were widely read as they appeared, and all except the last 8 were first printed in New York newspapers; the last 8 were first included in a two-volume edition of all the essays in 1788 and were then reprinted in the newspapers. Although the essays had little impact on the debate to ratify the Constitution, they are still considered a classic work of political theory. The authors expounded at length upon the fundamental problems of republican government, and argued that federalism offered a means of both preserving state sovereignty and safeguarding the individual's freedom from tyrannical rule. Many editions of the papers have been published and much has been written about them, a great deal of it devoted to determining authorship. (Columbia Encyclopedia)

II. Questions to think about as you read the text

1. What is Madison's argument against removing the causes of faction?
2. What according to Madison is the ultimate cause of different opinions of the people, which lead to faction?
3. Try to identify ideas of government from John Locke and Montesquieu in this paper.

III. Suggested essay topics

1. Is a utopian society of harmony possible or even desirable?
2. The pros and cons of majority rule from your own experience.

IV. Further reading

The Federal Convention of 1787

The Federal Convention of 1787 stands as a pivotal moment in the history of the United States, marking a critical turning point in the journey toward establishing a more perfect union. As the fledgling nation grappled with the inherent weaknesses of the Articles of Confederation, delegates from across the thirteen states gathered in Philadelphia to accomplish the momentous task of crafting a new framework for governance. Their deliberations and decisions during that summer ultimately gave birth to the United States Constitution, shaping the course of American history.

The Convention convened against a backdrop of political and economic challenges that threatened to undermine the stability and potential of the young nation. The weaknesses of the Articles of Confederation had become increasingly apparent, with a lack of centralized authority hampering effective governance and impeding the nation's ability to address pressing issues such as interstate trade, taxation, and national defense. It was clear that a more robust and cohesive system was needed to secure the future of the United States.

Delegates from diverse backgrounds and perspectives assembled under the leadership of luminaries such as George Washington, James Madison, Benjamin Franklin, and Alexander Hamilton. The Convention became a crucible of ideas, where the intellectual giants of the time debated and negotiated, striving to strike a delicate balance between liberty and order, between states' rights and a stronger central government.

The proceedings of the Convention were cloaked in secrecy, with delegates recognizing the sensitivity and gravity of the task before them. Closed doors allowed for frank discussions, free from the constraints of public opinion and political posturing. The debates revolved around core principles of governance, including the separation of powers, representation, and the division of authority between the federal and state governments.

Contentious issues, such as the balance between small and large states, the structure of the legislative branch, and the institution of slavery, sparked heated exchanges and fierce disagreements. Yet, through compromise and the spirit of collaboration, the delegates navigated these challenges, ultimately reaching consensus on a new blueprint for the nation.

The lasting legacy of the Federal Convention of 1787 cannot be overstated. The resulting Constitution established a durable framework for a federal republic, introducing a system of checks and balances, defining the powers and responsibilities of the three branches of government, and safeguarding individual rights through the *Bill of Rights*. It created a flexible and adaptable structure that has endured for over two centuries, allowing the nation to grow, evolve, and face the challenges of the future.

A Vindication of the Rights of Woman[1]

...

A man, when he undertakes a journey, has, in general, the end in view; a woman thinks more of the incidental occurrences, the strange things that may possibly occur on the road; the impression that she may make on her fellow-travellers; and, above all, she is anxiously intent on the care of the finery that she carries with her, which is more than ever a part of herself, when going to figure on a new scene; when, to use an apt French turn of expression, she is going to produce a sensation. — Can dignity of mind exist with such trivial cares?

In short, women, in general, as well as the rich of both sexes, have acquired all the follies and vices of civilization, and missed the useful fruit. It is not necessary for me always to premise, that I speak of the condition of the whole sex, leaving exceptions out of the question. Their senses are inflamed, and their understandings neglected, consequently they become the prey of their senses, delicately termed sensibility, and are blown about by every momentary gust of feeling. Civilized women are, therefore, so weakened

---

1 From *A Vindication of the Rights of Woman*, Chapter IV, by Mary Wollstonecraft, with minor editing.

by false refinement, that, respecting morals, their condition is much below what it would be were they left in a state nearer to nature. Ever restless and anxious, their over exercised sensibility not only renders them uncomfortable themselves, but troublesome, to use a soft phrase, to others. All their thoughts turn on things calculated to excite emotion; and feeling, when they should reason, their conduct is unstable, and their opinions are wavering — not the wavering produced by deliberation or progressive views, but by contradictory emotions. By fits and starts they are warm in many pursuits; yet this warmth, never concentrated into perseverance, soon exhausts itself; exhaled by its own heat, or meeting with some other fleeting passion, to which reason has never given any specific gravity, neutrality[1] ensues. Miserable, indeed, must be that being whose cultivation of mind has only tended to inflame its passions! A distinction should be made between inflaming and strengthening them. The passions thus pampered, whilst the judgment is left unformed, what can be expected to ensue? — Undoubtedly, a mixture of madness and folly!

This observation should not be confined to the fair sex; however, at present, I only mean to apply it to them.

Novels, music, poetry, and gallantry, all tend to make women the creatures of sensation, and their character is thus formed in the mould of folly during the time they are acquiring accomplishments, the only improvement they are excited, by their station in society, to acquire. This overstretched sensibility naturally relaxes the other powers of the mind, and prevents intellect from attaining that sovereignty which it ought to attain to render a rational creature useful to others, and content with its own station: for the exercise of the understanding, as life advances, is the only method pointed out by nature to calm the passions.

Satiety has a very different effect, and I have often been forcibly struck by an emphatical description of damnation: — when the spirit is represented

---

1   Neutrality, absence of decided views, feeling, or expression; indifference (OED).

as continually hovering with abortive eagerness round the defiled body, unable to enjoy anything without the organs of sense. Yet, to their senses, are women made slaves, because it is by their sensibility that they obtain present power.

And will moralists pretend to assert, that this is the condition in which one half of the human race should be encouraged to remain with listless inactivity and stupid acquiescence? Kind instructors! what were we created for? To remain, it may be said, innocent; they mean in a state of childhood. — We might as well never have been born, unless it were necessary that we should be created to enable man to acquire the noble privilege of reason, the power of discerning good from evil, whilst we lie down in the dust from whence we were taken, never to rise again. —

It would be an endless task to trace the variety of meannesses, cares, and sorrows, into which women are plunged by the prevailing opinion, that they were created rather to feel than reason, and that all the power they obtain, must be obtained by their charms and weakness:

> Fine by defect, and amiably weak![1]

And, made by this amiable weakness entirely dependent, excepting what they gain by illicit sway, on man, not only for protection, but advice, is it surprising that, neglecting the duties that reason alone points out, and shrinking from trials calculated to strengthen their minds, they only exert themselves to give their defects a graceful covering, which may serve to heighten their charms in the eye of the voluptuary, though it sinks them below the scale of moral excellence?

Fragile in every sense of the word, they are obliged to look up to man for every comfort. In the most trifling dangers they cling to their

---

1 "Fine by defect, and delicately weak," *Moral Essays* (2.43), by Alexander Pope.

support, with parasitical tenacity, piteously demanding succour; and their natural protector extends his arm, or lifts up his voice, to guard the lovely trembler — from what? Perhaps the frown of an old cow, or the jump of a mouse; a rat, would be a serious danger. In the name of reason, and even common sense, what can save such beings from contempt; even though they be soft and fair?

These fears, when not affected, may produce some pretty attitudes; but they shew a degree of imbecility which degrades a rational creature in a way women are not aware of — for love and esteem are very distinct things.

...

Ignorance is a frail base for virtue! Yet, that it is the condition for which woman was organized, has been insisted upon by the writers who have most vehemently argued in favour of the superiority of man; a superiority not in degree, but essence; though, to soften the argument, they have laboured to prove, with chivalrous generosity, that the sexes ought not to be compared; man was made to reason, woman to feel: and that together, flesh and spirit, they make the most perfect whole, by blending happily reason and sensibility into one character.

And what is sensibility? "Quickness of sensation; quickness of perception; delicacy." Thus is it defined by Dr. Johnson;[1] and the definition gives me no other idea than of the most exquisitely polished instinct. I discern not a trace of the image of God in either sensation or matter. Refined seventy times seven,[2] they are still material; intellect dwells not there; nor will fire ever make lead gold!

...

---

1 Samuel Johnson (1709–1784), English critic, biographer, essayist, poet, and lexicographer, known for his dictionary of the English language and regarded as one of the major figures of 18th-century life and letters.
2 Matthew 18.22: "Jesus saith unto him, I say not unto thee, Until seven times: but, Until seventy times seven."

With respect to women, when they receive a careful education, they are either made fine ladies, brimful of sensibility, and teeming with capricious fancies; or mere notable[1] women. The latter are often friendly, honest creatures, and have a shrewd kind of good sense joined with worldly prudence, that often render them more useful members of society than the fine sentimental lady, though they possess neither greatness of mind nor taste. The intellectual world is shut against them; take them out of their family or neighbourhood, and they stand still; the mind finding no employment, for literature affords a fund of amusement which they have never sought to relish, but frequently to despise. The sentiments and taste of more cultivated minds appear ridiculous, even in those whom chance and family connections have led them to love; but in mere acquaintance they think it all affectation ...

A fine lady ... has been taught to look down with contempt on the vulgar employments of life; though she has only been incited to acquire accomplishments that rise a degree above sense; for even corporeal accomplishments cannot be acquired with any degree of precision unless the understanding has been strengthened by exercise. Without a foundation of principles taste is superficial, grace must arise from something deeper than imitation. The imagination, however, is heated, and the feelings rendered fastidious, if not sophisticated; or, a counterpoise of judgment is not acquired, when the heart still remains artless, though it becomes too tender.

These women are often amiable; and their hearts are really more sensible to general benevolence, more alive to the sentiments that civilize life, than the square-elbowed family drudge; but, wanting a due proportion of reflection and self-government, they only inspire love; and are the mistresses of their husbands, whilst they have any hold on their affections; and the platonic friends of his male acquaintance. These are the fair defects in nature; the

---

1 Of women: Capable, managing, bustling; clever and industrious in household management or occupations [OED].

women who appear to be created not to enjoy the fellowship of man, but to save him from sinking into absolute brutality, by rubbing off the rough angles of his character; and by playful dalliance to give some dignity to the appetite that draws him to them. — Gracious Creator of the whole human race! hast thou created such a being as woman, who can trace thy wisdom in thy works, and feel that thou alone art by thy nature exalted above her, — for no better purpose? — Can she believe that she was only made to submit to man, her equal, a being, who, like her, was sent into the world to acquire virtue? — Can she consent to be occupied merely to please him; merely to adorn the earth, when her soul is capable of rising to thee? — And can she rest supinely dependent on man for reason, when she ought to mount with him the arduous steeps of knowledge? —

Yet, if love be the supreme good, let women be only educated to inspire it, and let every charm be polished to intoxicate the senses; but, if they be moral beings, let them have a chance to become intelligent; and let love to man be only a part of that glowing flame of universal love, which, after encircling humanity, mounts in grateful incense to God.

I. Supplementary information

Mary Wollstonecraft, an Early Feminist

Mary Wollstonecraft (1759–1797) was a British writer, philosopher, and champion of women's rights. She is best known for her groundbreaking work *A Vindication of the Rights of Woman*, which is considered one of the earliest feminist texts.

Born in London, England, Wollstonecraft grew up in a family that struggled with financial difficulties. Despite limited formal education, she developed a passion for learning and reading, which eventually led her to become a teacher and governess. In 1787, Wollstonecraft published her first major work, *Thoughts on the Education of Daughters*, which argued for equal education for both boys and girls. Her most influential work, *A Vindication of the Rights of Woman*, was published in 1792. In this seminal piece, Wollstonecraft argues that women were not inherently inferior to men but were rather denied equal opportunities due to social restrictions and their lack of education. She advocates women's access to education, employment, and political participation, challenging the prevailing views on gender roles and asserting that women should be seen as rational beings with the capacity for reason and intellectual growth.

Wollstonecraft's writings were met with both admiration and criticism during her lifetime. Her ideas were considered radical and controversial, as they challenged the traditional roles and expectations imposed on women. She argued for women's rights as human rights, paving the way for later feminist movements.

Mary Wollstonecraft was married to William Godwin, a prominent progressive thinker, with whom she had a daughter, the future Mary Shelley, author of *Frankenstein*. Tragically, Wollstonecraft's life was cut short at the age of thirty-eight due to complications following childbirth. However, her ideas continued to inspire generations of feminists and social reformers, and her work remains a significant contribution to the field of gender equality and women's rights.

II. Questions to think about as you read the text

1. In what ways is Wollstonecraft's view on gender roles similar to or different from today's feminist notions?
2. For Wollstonecraft, what was the root cause of women's condition in

her age? And what was her solution?

III. Suggested essay topics

1. There may be points in this excerpt about which you have reservations. Write an essay in response to Wollstonecraft on these points.
2. Write an essay on what you believe to be problems in the prevailing notions of femininity and masculinity in this society or any society familiar to you.

IV. Further reading

Sensibility

Much of Mary Wollstonecraft's book is a response to or a critique of a very important cultural concept in the 18th century, sensibility. According to the OED, in the 18th and early 19th centuries (afterwards somewhat rarely), sensibility referred to the capacity for refined emotion; delicate sensitiveness of taste; also, readiness to feel compassion for suffering, and to be moved by the pathetic in literature or art. Indeed, in Wollstonecraft's days, the term was often associated with a cultural and intellectual movement that emphasized heightened emotional sensitivity and sympathy.

Initially, sensibility was viewed as a desirable quality that elevated individuals above mere rationality. It lay at the centre of a culture that valued sentiment, emotions, and compassion in human interactions. Those who possessed sensibility were believed to have a deep capacity for feeling and an acute sensitivity to the suffering of others. This sensitivity was seen as a mark of moral virtue and refinement, in contrast with the cold rationality associated with the previous Age of Reason.

The literature and novels of the time often depicted characters with strong sensibility, who were portrayed as virtuous and capable of deep sympathy. These characters often experience profound emotional responses, and display a heightened sense of moral duty. The concept of sensibility also found expression in sentimental novels, which aimed to evoke strong emotional responses from readers and promote social reform by appealing to their compassion.

However, over time, the connotations of sensibility began to shift. Critics argued that excessive sentimentality and the cult of sensibility were leading to an overly emotional and irrational society. They criticized the sentimental novels for their exaggerated emotions and sentimentality, accusing them of indulging in shallow and manipulative portrayals of feeling. This shift in perception led to a decline in the popularity and influence of the sensibility movement. By the end of the 18th century, sensibility started to lose its prominent position in cultural and intellectual discourse.

The Imitation of Our Lord Don Quixote[1]

That Don Quixote[2] proved ultimately to have been wise is a point which was persuasively developed by [...] Mark Van Doren [...] in his essay *Don Quixote's Profession*.[3] This piece, now sadly out of print, deserves urgently to be rediscovered by all lovers of literature.

Van Doren aptly characterizes *Don Quixote* as a book of "mysterious simplicity": "The sign of its simplicity is that it can be summarized in a few sentences. The sign of its mysteriousness is that it can be talked about forever.

---

1 Excerpted from Simon Leys, "The Imitation of Our Lord Don Quixote," *The New York Review of Books*, June 11, 1998: 34–5. Copyright © 1998, Simon Leys. Reprinted with permission from original publisher.

2 Also spelled Don Quijote, 17th-century Spanish literary character, the protagonist of the prose fiction *Don Quixote* by Miguel de Cervantes. The book, originally published in Spanish in two parts (1605, 1615), concerns the eponymous would-be knight errant whose delusions of grandeur make him the butt of many practical jokes. *Don Quixote* is considered by literary historians to be one of the most important books of all time. The character of Quixote became an archetype, and the word quixotic, used to mean the impractical pursuit of idealistic goals, entered common usage.

3 *Don Quixote's Profession*, originally a series of three lectures, was first published as a monograph by Columbia University Press in 1958. It was subsequently reproduced in a collection of Van Doren's essays, *The Happy Critic* (Hill and Wang, 1961). This volume, like most of Van Doren's other writings, has now become extremely rare.

It has indeed been talked about as no other story ever was. For a strange thing happens to its readers. They do not read the same book ... . There were never so many theories about anything, one is tempted to say, as there are about *Don Quixote*. Yet it survives them all, as a masterpiece must do, if it would live."

The entire essay begins with a paragraph which deserves to be quoted in full, for, in its luminous elegance, it affords a characteristic example of Van Doren's style:

> A gentleman of fifty, with nothing to do, once invented for himself an occupation. Those about him, in his household and his village, were of the opinion that no such desperate step was necessary. He had an estate, and he was fond of hunting; these, they said, were occupation enough, and he should be content with the uneventful routines it imposed. But the gentleman was not content. And when he set out in earnest to live an altogether different life he was thought by everybody, first at home and then abroad, to be either strange or mad. He went away three times, returning once of his own accord, but in the second and third cases being brought back by persons of the village who had pursued him for this purpose. He returned each time in an exhausted state, for the occupation he embraced was strenuous; and soon after his third homecoming he took to bed, made his will, confessed his sins, admitted that the whole enterprise had been an error, and died.

The central argument in Van Doren's essay is that (whatever Cervantes himself may have thought on the subject) Don Quixote was not mad. He became deluded only when he tried to assess the progress of his enterprise. And here, the hoaxes to which he fell victim played a fatal role: they gave him a false assurance that his undertaking was really feasible, they confirmed his mistaken hope that he might eventually succeed. Thus, these hoaxes artificially prolonged his career. Yet, at any time he could have abandoned his quest and returned home, had success not appeared to be within reach. Only the illusion which fed on the hoaxes gave him the courage to forge ahead. But he always remained free to decide whether to pursue or to desist. A real madman does not have such a choice: he is the prisoner of his madness; when it becomes unbearable he cannot drop out of it and simply go home to resume his previous way of life.

The occupation which Don Quixote chooses for himself is that of knight errant. He is not under the delusion that he is a knight errant—no, he sets his mind on *becoming* one. He does not play at being someone else, as children do in their games; he is not pretending to be someone else, like an imposter, or impersonating a character, like an actor on stage. And he adopts the profession of knight after due reflection: it is the result of a deliberate choice. After having considered other options, he finally decided that the career of a knight errant would be the most rewarding, intellectually and morally.

But how does one become a knight? Van Doren asks. By acting like a knight — which is the very opposite of pretense, of make-believe. And to act the way Don Quixote does is more than to ape. To imitate as he does is a profound apprenticeship — the true way of learning and the key to understanding. "What is the difference between acting like a great man and being one?" Van Doren asks. "To act like a poet is to write poems; to act like a statesman is to ponder the nature of goodness and justice; to act like a student is to study; to act like a knight is to think and feel like one."

Had Don Quixote been simply and plainly mad, or had he indulged in a protracted game of self-deception and play-acting, we should not be talking of him now, Van Doren observes—"We are talking of him because we suspect that, in the end, he did become a knight."

"Man is a creature who makes pictures of himself, and then comes to resemble the picture." Iris Murdoch made this observation in a different context, but it accurately identifies a defining feature of human nature. It was most memorably exemplified by Don Quixote—which gave Cervantes' novel its universal relevance.

Unlike Don Quixote, however, most of us do not have the chance to select and decide for ourselves which characters we should apply ourselves to becoming. Circumstances of life do the casting; our roles are being imposed on us, other people dictate to us our lines and prompt our acting. A haunting illustration of this was provided in one of Rossellini's[1] last films, *General della Rovere* (1959). A petty crook in Italy at the end of World War II is arrested by the Gestapo and forced by them to impersonate a prestigious figure of the Resistance, General della Rovere, so that they can extract information from political prisoners. But the con man performs his role so convincingly that the other prisoners come to worship him as their moral leader; thus he is progressively compelled to live above himself and to match the image created by their expectations. In the end, he refused to betray their trust; he is put in front of the firing squad and dies the death of a hero. He has truly become General della Rovere.

As for us, life seldom offers such dramatic scripts. Usually the roles we have to play are more humble and banal — which does not mean that they are less heroic. We too have companions of captivity with extravagant expectations that can force us to enact parts well beyond our natural abilities. Our parents expect us to be sons or daughters, our children expect us to be fathers and mothers, our spouses expect us to be husbands and wives; and none of these roles is light or easy. They are all fraught with risks and challenges, with trials, anguishes, humiliations, with victories and defeats.

To the basic interrogation of man: Why is it that God never speaks to us openly or answers us directly with a clear voice? Why are we never allowed to see his face? C. S. Lewis gave a striking answer: How can God meet us

---

1   Robert Rossellini (1906–1977), one of the most widely known post-World War II motion-picture directors of Italy. His films *Roma città aperta* (1945; *Open City*) and *Paisà* (1946; *Paisan*) focused international attention on the Italian Neorealist movement in films.

face to face, *till we have faces*?

When we first enter upon the stage of life, it is as if we were only given masks that correspond to our respective roles. If we act our part well enough the mask eventually turns into our true face. Thus Don Quixote becomes a knight, Rossellini's petty crook becomes General della Rovere — and each of us, we can become at last who we were originally meant to be.

The famous multibillionaire Ted Turner made a remarkable statement some years ago. He said he disliked Christianity, as he felt that it was "a religion of losers." How very true! What an accurate definition indeed!

The word "quixotic" [...] has entered the common language, with the meaning "hopelessly naïve and idealistic," "ridiculously impractical," "doomed to fail." That this epithet can be used now in an exclusively pejorative sense not only shows that we have ceased to read Cervantes and to understand his character, but more fundamentally it reveals that our culture has drifted away from its spiritual roots.

Make no mistake: for all its earthiness, its cynical jests, its bawdy and scatological realism, Cervantes' masterpiece is anchored in Christianity — more specifically, in Spanish Catholicism, with its strong mystical drive. In this very connection, Unamuno[1] remarked that John of the Cross, Teresa of Avila, and Ignatius of Loyola did not reject rationality, nor did they distrust scientific knowledge; what led them to their mysticism was simply the perception of *"an intolerable disparity between the hugeness of their desire and the smallness of reality."*

In his quest for immortal fame, Don Quixote suffered repeated defeats. Because he obstinately refused to adjust "the hugeness of his desire" to "the smallness of reality," he was doomed to perpetual failure. Only a culture based upon "a religion of losers" could produce such a hero.

---

1 Miguel de Unamuno. Unamuno (1864–1936) was a multiform genius: scholar, philosopher, novelist, essayist, poet — Basque, Spaniard, European, universal humanist.

What we should remember, however, is this (if I may thus paraphrase Bernard Shaw): The successful man adapts himself to the world. The loser persists in trying to adapt the world to himself. Therefore all progress depends on the loser.

I. Supplementary information

1. Chivalry

The word chivalry often refers to the skills and qualities expected of a knight. It encompassed a set of chief virtues, including piety, honor, valor, courtesy, chastity, and loyalty. The knight's loyalty extended to three entities: their spiritual master, God; their temporal master, the suzerain; and their beloved, whom they held in their heart. Chivalrous love, in most cases, was platonic, limited usually to a woman of a higher social position, as we have already discussed earlier in this book.

2. Chivalry and Religion

During the Middle Ages, warfare was a constant presence, and knights and soldiers held significant power and influence. However, this power also carried the potential for abuse and disruption of social order. Christianity was instrumental in channeling and tempering the violent tendencies of medieval soldiers, providing a framework of moral and ethical guidelines through which their behavior could be regulated.

The medieval Christian belief system instilled a sense of divine authority and divine judgment. Soldiers were taught that their actions and conduct would be judged by God, and that they had a responsibility to act in accordance with God's will. This belief in divine judgment served as a deterrent and reminded soldiers of the consequences of misconduct.

Religion provided a moral framework within which chivalry operated. Christian teachings attached great importance to virtues such as humility, mercy, justice, and compassion. Knights were expected to embody these virtues and apply them in their interactions with others, including enemies. Religion taught soldiers to treat captives and non-combatants with respect and to follow ethical principles even in the chaos of war.

Religious orders and institutions played a vital role in establishing and enforcing codes of conduct for knights and soldiers. These codes, such as the Code of Chivalry, often drew inspiration from Christian teachings and ideals. Knights were expected to adhere to principles such as protecting the weak, defending the faith, and fighting with honor. Violations of these codes could result in spiritual consequences, including excommunication from the Church.

Religious ceremonies and rituals were integrated into the life of a knight, emphasizing the spiritual dimension of their role. Knights took oaths and vows before religious figures or on religious relics, adding a sacred element to their commitment to chivalry. These rituals reinforced the religious aspect of their code of conduct and further bound them to their moral obligations.

3. Mysticism

There are certain common fallacies current about mysticism: that mystics are not "practical" and that they are revolutionary; on the contrary, many of the greatest mystics have been both intensely active as well as submissive to authority of whatever sort. Nor is the "solitary thinker" necessarily, or even usually, a mystic. There is no accepted explanation of mysticism, and few psychologists have interested themselves in its practice.

There are two general tendencies in the speculation of mystics — to regard God as outside the soul, which rises to its God by successive stages, or to regard God as dwelling within the soul and to be found by delving deeper into one's own reality. The idea of transcendence, as held most firmly by mystics, is the kernel of the ancient mystical system, Neoplatonism, and of Gnosticism. Their explanation of the connection between God and humans by emanation is epoch-making in the philosophy of contemplation. Among those who think of God, or the Supreme Reality, as being within the soul are the Quakers and the adherents of Vedanta.

II. Questions to think about as you read the text

1. What, according to this article, underlies Don Quixote's desire to live the life of a knight?
2. What does the notion of "loser" mean in the article? And what does the author mean by "successful"?
3. What is the connection between mysticism/mystics and Don Quixote's desire to be a knight?

III. Suggested essay topics

1. Steve Jobs has a talk with Don Quixote.
2. How Don Quixote would fare in China.

IV. Further reading

The Office of a Knight[1]

The office of a knight is to maintain and defend his lord worldly or earthly, for a king nor no high baron hath no power to maintain right in his men without aid and help. Then if any man do against the commandment of his king or prince, it behooveth that the knights aid their lord ..., and therefore the evil knight which sooner helpeth another man that would put down his lord from the seignory that

---

[1] From Ramon Llull, *The Book of the Ordre of Chyualry*, tr. by William Caxton (Oxford: Oxford University Press, 1926).

he ought to have upon him, he followeth not the office by which he is called a knight. By the knights ought to be maintained and kept justice ... Knights ought to take coursers to joust and to go to tourneys, to hold open table, to hunt at harts, boars and other wild beasts. For in doing these things the knights exercize them to arms for to maintain the order of knighthood ... And thus, as all these things aforesaid pertain to a knight as touching his body, in like wise justice, wisdom, charity, loyalty, truth, humility, strength, hope, swiftness and all other virtues similarly pertain to a knight as touching his soul, and therefore the knight that useth the things that pertain to the order of chivalry as touching his body, and hath none of these virtues that pertain to chivalry touching his soul is not the friend of the order of knighthood ...

The office of a knight is to maintain the land, for because that the dread of the common people have of the knights, they labor and cultivate the earth for fear lest they should be destroyed. And by the dread of the knights they fear the kings, princes and lords by whom they have their power ...

The office of a knight is to maintain and defend women, widows and orphans, and men diseased and not puissant nor strong. For like as custom and reason is that the greatest and most mighty help the feeble and less, and that they have recourse to the great, right so is the order of chivalry, because she is great, honorable and mighty, be in succor and in aid to them that be under him, and less mighty and less honored than he is ...

The office of a knight is to have a castle and horse for to keep the highways, and for to defend them that labor on the lands and the earth, and they ought to have towns and cities for to hold right [administer justice] to the people, and for to assemble in a place men of many diverse crafts, which be much necessary to the ordinance of this world to keep and maintain the life of man and of woman.

Of Individuality[1]

In sober truth, whatever homage may be professed, or even paid, to real or supposed mental superiority, the general tendency of things throughout the world is to render mediocrity the ascendant power among mankind. In ancient history, in the Middle Ages, and in a diminishing degree through the long transition from feudality to the present time, the individual was a power in himself; and if he had either great talents or a high social position, he was a considerable power. At present individuals are lost in the crowd. In politics it is almost a triviality to say that public opinion now rules the world. The only power deserving the name is that of masses, and of governments while they make themselves the organ of the tendencies and instincts of masses. This is as true in the moral and social relations of private life as in public transactions. Those whose opinions go by the name of public opinion, are not always the same sort of public: in America, they are the whole white population; in England, chiefly the middle class. But they are always a mass, that is to say, collective mediocrity. And what is still greater novelty, the mass do not now take their opinions from dignitaries in Church or State, from ostensible leaders, or from books. Their thinking is done for them by

---

1 From John Stuart Mill, *On Liberty*.

men much like themselves, addressing them or speaking in their name, on the spur of the moment, through the newspapers. I am not complaining of all this. I do not assert that anything better is compatible, as a general rule, with the present low state of the human mind. But that does not hinder the government of mediocrity from being mediocre government. No government by a democracy or a numerous aristocracy, either in its political acts or in the opinions, qualities, and tone of mind which it fosters, ever did or could rise above mediocrity, except in so far as the sovereign Many have let themselves be guided (which in their best times they always have done) by the counsels and influence of a more highly gifted and instructed One or Few. The initiation of all wise or noble things, comes and must come from individuals; generally at first from some one individual. The honor and glory of the average man is that he is capable of following that initiative; that he can respond internally to wise and noble things, and be led to them with his eyes open. I am not countenancing the sort of "hero-worship"[1] which applauds the strong man of genius for forcibly seizing on the government of the world and making it do his bidding in spite of itself. All he can claim is, freedom to point out the way. The power of compelling others into it, is not only inconsistent with the freedom and development of all the rest, but corrupting to the strong man himself. It does seem, however, that when the opinions of masses of merely average men are everywhere become or becoming the dominant power, the counterpoise and corrective to that tendency would be, the more and more pronounced individuality of those who stand on the higher eminences of thought. It is in these circumstances most especially, that exceptional individuals, instead of being deterred, should be encouraged in acting differently from the mass. In other times there was no advantage in

---

1 Thomas Carlyle (1795–1881), English author, known for his notion of hero worship. His lectures, published as *On Heroes, Hero-Worship, and the Heroic in History* (1841), express his view that the great men of the past have intuitively shaped destiny and have been the spiritual leaders of the world.

their doing so, unless they acted not only differently, but better. In this age the mere example of nonconformity, the mere refusal to bend the knee to custom, is itself a service. Precisely because the tyranny of opinion is such as to make eccentricity a reproach, it is desirable, in order to break through that tyranny, that people should be eccentric. Eccentricity has always abounded when and where strength of character has abounded; and the amount of eccentricity in a society has generally been proportional to the amount of genius, mental vigor, and moral courage which it contained. That so few now dare to be eccentric, marks the chief danger of the time.

I have said that it is important to give the freest scope possible to uncustomary things, in order that it may in time appear which of these are fit to be converted into customs. But independence of action, and disregard of custom are not solely deserving of encouragement for the chance they afford that better modes of action, and customs more worthy of general adoption, may be struck out; nor is it only persons of decided mental superiority who have a just claim to carry on their lives in their own way. There is no reason that all human existences should be constructed on some one, or some small number of patterns. If a person possesses any tolerable amount of common sense and experience, his own mode of laying out his existence is the best, not because it is the best in itself, but because it is his own mode. Human beings are not like sheep; and even sheep are not undistinguishably alike. A man cannot get a coat or a pair of boots to fit him, unless they are either made to his measure, or he has a whole warehouseful to choose from: and is it easier to fit him with a life than with a coat, or are human beings more like one another in their whole physical and spiritual conformation than in the shape of their feet? If it were only that people have diversities of taste that is reason enough for not attempting to shape them all after one model. But different persons also require different conditions for their spiritual development; and can no more exist healthily in the same moral, than all the variety of plants can in the same physical atmosphere and climate. The same things which are helps to one person towards the cultivation of his higher nature, are hindrances to another. The same mode of life is a healthy excitement to one, keeping all his faculties of action and enjoyment in their best order, while to another it is a distracting burden, which suspends or crushes all internal life. Such are the differences among human beings in their sources of pleasure, their susceptibilities of pain, and the operation on them of different physical and moral agencies, that unless there is a corresponding diversity in their modes of life, they neither obtain their fair share of happiness, nor grow up to the mental, moral, and aesthetic stature of which their nature is capable. Why then should tolerance, as far as the public sentiment is concerned, extend only to tastes and modes of life which extort acquiescence by the multitude of their adherents? Nowhere (except in some monastic institutions) is diversity of taste entirely unrecognized; a person may without blame, either like or dislike rowing, or smoking, or music, or athletic exercises, or chess, or cards, or study, because both those who like each of these things, and those who dislike them, are too numerous to be put down. But the man, and still more the woman, who can be accused either of doing "what nobody does," or of not doing "what everybody does," is the subject of as much depreciatory remark as if he or she had committed some grave moral delinquency. Persons require to possess a title, or some other badge of rank, or the consideration of people of rank, to be able to indulge somewhat in the luxury of doing as they like without detriment to their estimation. To indulge somewhat, I repeat: for whoever allow themselves much of that indulgence, incur the risk of something worse than disparaging speeches — they are in peril of a commission *de lunatico*[1], and of having their property taken from them and given to their relations.

---

1 Of the sanity of a person. Commission of Lunacy: this refers to a writ issued by chancery, or such court as may have jurisdiction over the case directed to a proper officer, to inquire whether a person named therein is a lunatic or not.

...

The despotism of custom is everywhere the standing hindrance to human advancement, being in unceasing antagonism to that disposition to aim at something better than customary, which is called, according to circumstances, the spirit of liberty, or that of progress or improvement. The spirit of improvement is not always a spirit of liberty, for it may aim at forcing improvements on an unwilling people; and the spirit of liberty, in so far as it resists such attempts, may ally itself locally and temporarily with the opponents of improvement; but the only unfailing and permanent source of improvement is liberty, since by it there are as many possible independent centres of improvement as there are individuals. The progressive principle, however, in either shape, whether as the love of liberty or of improvement, is antagonistic to the sway of Custom, involving at least emancipation from that yoke; and the contest between the two constitutes the chief interest of the history of mankind. The greater part of the world has, properly speaking, no history, because the despotism of Custom is complete. This is the case over the whole East. Custom is there, in all things, the final appeal; Justice and right mean conformity to custom; the argument of custom no one, unless some tyrant intoxicated with power, thinks of resisting. And we see the result. Those nations must once have had originality; they did not start out of the ground populous, lettered, and versed in many of the arts of life; they made themselves all this, and were then the greatest and most powerful nations in the world. What are they now? The subjects or dependents of tribes whose forefathers wandered in the forests when theirs had magnificent palaces and gorgeous temples, but over whom custom exercised only a divided rule with liberty and progress. A people, it appears, may be progressive for a certain length of time, and then stop: when does it stop? When it ceases to possess individuality. If a similar change should befall the nations of Europe, it will not be in exactly the same shape: the despotism of custom with which these nations are threatened is not precisely stationariness. It proscribes singularity, but it does not preclude change, provided all change together. We have discarded the fixed costumes of our forefathers; every one must still dress like other people, but the fashion may change once or twice a year. We thus take care that when there is change, it shall be for change's sake, and not from any idea of beauty or convenience; for the same idea of beauty or convenience would not strike all the world at the same moment, and be simultaneously thrown aside by all at another moment. But we are progressive as well as changeable: we continually make new inventions in mechanical things, and keep them until they are again superseded by better; we are eager for improvement in politics, in education, even in morals, though in this last our idea of improvement chiefly consists in persuading or forcing other people to be as good as ourselves. It is not progress that we object to; on the contrary, we flatter ourselves that we are the most progressive people who ever lived. It is individuality that we war against: we should think we had done wonders if we had made ourselves all alike; forgetting that the unlikeness of one person to another is generally the first thing which draws the attention of either to the imperfection of his own type, and the superiority of another, or the possibility, by combining the advantages of both, of producing something better than either. We have a warning example in China — a nation of much talent, and, in some respects, even wisdom, owing to the rare good fortune of having been provided at an early period with a particularly good set of customs, the work, in some measure, of men to whom even the most enlightened European must accord, under certain limitations, the title of sages and philosophers. They are remarkable, too, in the excellence of their apparatus for impressing, as far as possible, the best wisdom they possess upon every mind in the community, and securing that those who have appropriated most of it shall occupy the posts of honor and power. Surely the people who did this have discovered the secret of human progressiveness, and must have kept themselves steadily at the head of the movement of the world. On the contrary, they have become stationary —

have remained so for thousands of years; and if they are ever to be farther improved, it must be by foreigners. They have succeeded beyond all hope in what English philanthropists are so industriously working at — in making a people all alike, all governing their thoughts and conduct by the same maxims and rules; and these are the fruits. The modern regime of public opinion is, in an unorganized form, what the Chinese educational and political systems are in an organized; and unless individuality shall be able successfully to assert itself against this yoke, Europe, notwithstanding its noble antecedents and its professed Christianity, will tend to become another China.

I. Supplementary information

1. John Stuart Mill

John Stuart Mill (1806–1873), English philosopher, economist, and exponent of utilitarianism. He was prominent as a publicist in the reforming age of the 19th century, and remains of lasting interest as a logician and an ethical theorist. Mill was raised by social reformers — his father, James Mill (1773–1836), and Jeremy Bentham. His social theory was an attempt, by gradual means arrived at democratically, to combat the evils of the Industrial Revolution. His ethics, expressed in his *Utilitarianism* (1861), followed the formulations of Bentham in finding the end of society to consist in the production of the greatest quantity of happiness for its members, but he gave to Bentham's cruder (but more consistent) doctrines a humanistic and individualistic slant. Thus, the moral self-development of the individual becomes the ultimate value in Mill's ethics.

This trend was also expressed in his essays *On Liberty* (1859) and

Considerations on Representative Government (1861). In the former he stated the case for the freedom of the individual against "the tyranny of the majority," presented strong arguments in favour of complete freedom of thought and discussion, and argued that no state or society has the right to prevent the free development of human individuality. In the latter he provided a classic defense for the principle of representative democracy, asked for the adequate representation of minorities, urged renewed public participation in political action for necessary social reforms, and pointed out the dangers of class-oriented, or special-interest, legislation. (from Britannica)

2. Liberalism and utilitarianism

In the late 18th and early 19th centuries, Bentham, the philosopher James Mill, and James's son John Stuart Mill applied classical economic principles to the political sphere. Invoking the doctrine of utilitarianism — which asserts that an action is right if it tends to promote the happiness not only of the agent but of everyone affected by his act — they argued that the object of all legislation should be "the greatest happiness of the greatest number." In evaluating what kind of government could best attain this objective, the utilitarians generally supported representative democracy, asserting that it was the best way to make the interest of government coincide with the general interest. Taking their cue from the notion of a free-market economy, the utilitarians called for a political system that would guarantee its citizens the maximum degree of individual freedom of choice and action consistent with efficient government and the preservation of social harmony. They advocated expanded education, enlarged suffrage, and periodic elections to ensure government's accountability to the governed. They also developed a doctrine of individual rights — including the rights to freedom of religion, freedom of speech, freedom of the press, and freedom of assembly — that lies at the heart of modern democracy. These rights received their classic advocacy in John Stuart Mill's essay *On Liberty* (1859), which argues on utilitarian grounds that the state may regulate individual behaviour only in cases where the interests of others would be perceptibly harmed. Today, this work is justly celebrated as one of the great testimonials to civil liberties and a classic of liberal thought.

The utilitarians thus succeeded in broadening the philosophical foundations of political liberalism while also providing a program of specific reformist goals for liberals to pursue. Their overall political philosophy was perhaps best stated in James Mill's article "Government," which was written for the supplement (1815–24) to the fourth through sixth editions of the *Encyclopædia Britannica*. (Britannica)

3. Liberalism and democracy

Politically, liberalism ultimately aspired to a system of government based on majority rule — i.e., one in which government executed the expressed will of a majority of the electorate. The chief institutional devices for attaining this goal were the periodic election of legislators by popular vote and the election of a chief executive by popular vote or by a legislative assembly.

But in answering the crucial question of who is to be the electorate, classical liberalism fell victim to ambivalence, torn between the great emancipating tendencies generated by the revolutions with which it was associated and middle-class fears that a wide or universal franchise would undermine private property. Benjamin Franklin spoke for the Whig liberalism of the founding fathers of the United States when he stated, "As to those who have not landed property the allowing them to vote is an impropriety." John Adams, in his *Defense of the Constitutions of Government of the United States of America* (1787), was more explicit, finding that, if the majority were to control all branches of government, "Debts would be abolished first; taxes laid heavy on the rich, and not at all on others; and at last a downright equal division of everything be demanded and voted." French statesmen such as François Guizot and Adolphe Thiers expressed similar sentiments well into the 19th century.

Most 18th- and 19th-century liberal spokesmen thus feared popular sovereignty, and for a long time suffrage was limited to property owners. In Britain even the important Reform Act of 1867 did not completely abolish property qualifications for the right to vote. In France, although the Revolution of 1789 proclaimed the ideal of universal manhood suffrage and the July Revolution of 1830 reaffirmed it, there were no more than 200,000 qualified voters in a population of about 30 million during the reign of Louis-Philippe, the "citizen king" installed by the ascendant bourgeoisie in 1830. In the United States, Thomas Jefferson's brave language in the Declaration of Independence notwithstanding, it was not until 1860 that universal white male suffrage prevailed. In most of Europe universal male suffrage remained a remote ideal until late in the 19th century.

Despite the misgivings of the propertied classes, a slow but steady expansion of the franchise prevailed throughout Europe in the 19th century. But the principle of majority rule also had to be reconciled with the liberal requirement that the power of the majority be a limited one. The problem was to accomplish this in a manner consistent with the democratic ideal. Given that hereditary elites were discredited, how could the power of the majority be checked without giving disproportionate power to property owners or to some other "natural" élite? (Britannica)

II. Questions to think about as you read the text

1. In defending individuals' choice of way of life, Mill in fact goes through an important change in this article. Explain this change.
2. Does Mill make a distinction between social well-being or individual freedom in his argument for individuality? To which does he seem to

give more weight?

III. Suggested essay topics

1. Safety of the crowd.
2. How the illusion of public opinion works through social media?

IV. Further reading

Following are two more passages from the writings of Mill, both explicating his liberal views, one on individuality, the other on gender. Please note one common concern in these passages.

1. From *On Liberty*

Like other tyrannies, the tyranny of the majority was at first, and is still vulgarly, held in dread, chiefly as operating through the acts of the public authorities. But reflecting persons perceived that when society is itself the tyrant — society collectively, over the separate individuals who compose it — its means of tyrannizing are not restricted to the acts which it may do by the hands of its political functionaries. Society can and does execute its own mandates: and if it issues wrong mandates instead of right, or any mandates at all in things with which it ought not to meddle, it practises a social tyranny more formidable than many kinds of political oppression, since, though not usually upheld by such extreme penalties, it leaves fewer means of escape, penetrating much more deeply into the details of life, and enslaving the soul itself. Protection, therefore, against the tyranny of the magistrate is not enough; there needs protection also against the tyranny of the prevailing opinion and feeling; against the tendency of society to impose, by other means than civil penalties, its own ideas and practices as rules of conduct on those who dissent from them; to fetter the development, and, if possible, prevent the formation, of any individuality not in harmony with its ways, and compel all characters to fashion themselves upon the model of its own. There is a limit to the legitimate interference of collective opinion with individual independence; and to find that limit, and maintain it against encroachment, is as indispensable to a good condition of human affairs, as protection against political despotism.

2. From "The Subjection of Women"

... The subjection of women to men being a universal custom, any departure from it quite naturally appears unnatural. But how entirely, even in this case, the feeling is dependent on custom, appears by ample experience. Nothing so much astonishes the people of distant parts of the world, when they first learn anything about England, as to be told that it is under a queen: the thing seems to them so unnatural as to be almost incredible. To Englishmen this does not seem in the least degree unnatural, because they are used to it; but they do feel it unnatural that women should be soldiers or members of parliament. In the feudal ages, on the contrary, war and politics were not thought unnatural to women, because not unusual; it seemed natural that women of the privileged classes should be of manly character, inferior in nothing but bodily strength to their husbands and fathers. The independence of women seemed rather less unnatural to the Greeks than to other ancients, on account of the fabulous Amazons (whom they believed to be historical), and the partial example afforded by the Spartan women; who, though no less subordinate by law than in other Greek states, were more free in fact, and being trained to bodily exercises in the same manner with men, gave ample proof that they were not naturally disqualified for them. There can be little doubt that Spartan experience suggested to Plato, among many other of his doctrines, that of the social and political equality of the two sexes.

The Natural History of German Life[1]

...

Probably, if we could ascertain the images called up by the terms "the people," "the masses," "the proletariat," "the peasantry," by many who theorize on those bodies with eloquence, or who legislate for them without eloquence, we should find that they indicate almost as small an amount of concrete knowledge — that they are as far from completely representing the complex facts summed up in the collective term, as the railway images of our non-locomotive gentleman. How little the real characteristics of the working-classes are known to those who are outside them, how little their natural history has been studied, is sufficiently disclosed by our Art as well as by our political and social theories. Where, in our picture exhibitions, shall we find a group of true peasantry? What English artist even attempts to rival in truthfulness such studies of popular life as the pictures of Teniers[2]

---

1   Excerpted from George Eliot, "The Natural History of German Life," *The Westminster Review* (July 1856), Vol. 66 (old series), 10 (new series), pp. 51–79, with minor editing.
2   David Teniers the Younger, 1610–1690, noted Flemish genre painter, worked with his father in Antwerp. His early works show the influence of Bruegel the Elder, his father-in-law. A protégé of Rubens, Teniers became court painter to the governor of the Netherlands and also worked for Philip IV of Spain. Heavily commissioned, he painted a prodigious number of small, very finished pictures. His favorite subjects were quiet scenes from peasant life.

or the ragged boys of Murillo¹? Even one of the greatest painters of the pre-eminently realistic school, while, in his picture of "The Hireling Shepherd," he gave us a landscape of marvellous truthfulness, placed a pair of peasants in the foreground who were not much more real than the idyllic swains and damsels of our chimney ornaments. Only a total absence of acquaintance and sympathy with our peasantry, could give a moment's popularity to such a picture as "Cross Purposes," where we have a peasant girl who looks as if she knew L. E. L.'s² poems by heart, and English rustics, whose costume seems to indicate that they are meant for ploughmen, with exotic features that remind us of a handsome *primo tenore*³. Rather than such cockney sentimentality as this, as an education for the taste and sympathies, we prefer the most crapulous group of boors that Teniers ever painted. But even those among our painters who aim at giving the rustic type of features, who are far above the effeminate feebleness of the "Keepsake" style, treat their subjects under the influence of traditions and prepossessions rather than of direct observation. The notion that peasants are joyous, that the typical moment to represent a man in a smock-frock is when he is cracking a joke and showing a row of sound teeth, that cottage matrons are usually buxom, and village children necessarily rosy and merry, are prejudices difficult to dislodge from the artistic mind, which looks for its subjects into literature instead of life. The painter is still under the influence of idyllic literature, which has always expressed the imagination of the cultivated and town-bred, rather than the truth of rustic life. Idyllic ploughmen are jocund when they drive their team afield; idyllic shepherds make bashful love under hawthorn bushes; idyllic villagers dance in the chequered shade and refresh themselves, not immoderately, with spicy nut-brown ale. But no one who has seen much of

---

1 Bartolomé Esteban Murillo (1617?–1682), Spanish religious and portrait painter.
2 Probably refers to Letitia Elizabeth Landon (1802–1838), English poet and novelist who, at a time when women were conventionally restricted in their themes, wrote of passionate love.
3 Chief tenor singer.

actual ploughmen thinks them jocund; no one who is well acquainted with the English peasantry can pronounce them merry. The slow gaze, in which no sense of beauty beams, no humour twinkles, — the slow utterance, and the heavy slouching walk, remind one rather of that melancholy animal the camel, than of the sturdy countryman, with striped stockings, red waistcoat, and hat aside, who represents the traditional English peasant. Observe a company of haymakers. When you see them at a distance, tossing up the forkfuls of hay in the golden light, while the wagon creeps slowly with its increasing burthen over the meadow, and the bright green space which tells of work done gets larger and larger, you pronounce the scene "smiling," and you think these companions in labour must be as bright and cheerful as the picture to which they give animation. Approach nearer, and you will certainly find that haymaking time is a time for joking, especially if there are women among the labourers; but the coarse laugh that bursts out every now and then, and expresses the triumphant taunt, is as far as possible from your conception of idyllic merriment. That delicious effervescence of the mind which we call fun, has no equivalent for the northern peasant, except tipsy revelry; the only realm of fancy and imagination for the English clown exists at the bottom of the third quart pot.

The conventional countryman of the stage, who picks up pocket-books and never looks into them, and who is too simple even to know that honesty has its opposite, represents the still lingering mistake, that an unintelligible dialect is a guarantee for ingenuousness, and that slouching shoulders indicate an upright disposition. It is quite true that a thresher is likely to be innocent of any adroit arithmetical cheating, but he is not the less likely to carry home his master's corn in his shoes and pocket; a reaper is not given to writing begging-letters, but he is quite capable of cajoling the dairymaid into filling his small-beer bottle with ale. The selfish instincts are not subdued by the sight of buttercups, nor is integrity in the least established by that classic rural occupation, sheep-washing. To make men moral, something more is requisite than to turn them out to grass.

Opera peasants, whose unreality excites Mr. Ruskin's[1] indignation, are surely too frank an idealization to be misleading; and since popular chorus is one of the most effective elements of the opera, we can hardly object to lyric rustics in elegant laced bodices and picturesque motley, unless we are prepared to advocate a chorus of colliers in their pit costume, or a ballet of char-women and stocking-weavers. But our social novels profess to represent the people as they are, and the unreality of their representations is a grave evil. The greatest benefit we owe to the artist, whether painter, poet, or novelist, is the extension of our sympathies. Appeals founded on generalizations and statistics require a sympathy ready-made, a moral sentiment already in activity; but a picture of human life such as a great artist can give, surprises even the trivial and the selfish into that attention to what is apart from themselves, which may be called the raw material of moral sentiment. When Scott takes us into Luckie Mucklebackit's[2] cottage, or tells the story of "The Two Drovers," — when Wordsworth sings to us the reverie of "Poor Susan," — when Kingsley[3] shows us Alton Locke gazing yearningly over the gate which leads from the highway into the first wood he ever saw, — when Hornung[4] paints a group of chimney-sweepers, — more is done towards linking the higher classes with the lower, towards obliterating the vulgarity of exclusiveness, than by hundreds of sermons and philosophical dissertations. Art is the nearest thing to life; it is a mode of amplifying experience and extending our contact with our fellow-men beyond the bounds of our personal lot. All the more sacred is the task of the artist when he undertakes to paint the life of the People. Falsification here

---

1 John Ruskin (1819–1900), a British art critic and social critic, author of many essays including *Modern Painters*.
2 A character in the novel *The Antiquary* by Sir Walter Scott.
3 Charles Kingsley (1819–1875), English clergyman and novelist.
4 Joseph Hornung (1791–1870), Swiss painter.

is far more pernicious than in the more artificial aspects of life. It is not so very serious that we should have false ideas about evanescent fashions — about the manners and conversation of beaux and duchesses; but it is serious that our sympathy with the perennial joys and struggles, the toil, the tragedy, and the humour in the life of our more heavily-laden fellow-men, should be perverted, and turned towards a false object instead of the true one.

This perversion is not the less fatal because the misrepresentation which gives rise to it has what the artist considers a moral end. The thing for mankind to know is, not what are the motives and influences which the moralist thinks ought to act on the labourer or the artisan, but what are the motives and influences which do act on him. We want to be taught to feel, not for the heroic artisan or the sentimental peasant, but for the peasant in all his coarse apathy, and the artisan in all his suspicious selfishness.

We have one great novelist who is gifted with the utmost power of rendering the external traits of our town population; and if he could give us their psychological character — their conceptions of life, and their emotions — with the same truth as their idiom and manners, his books would be the greatest contribution Art has ever made to the awakening of social sympathies. But while he can copy Mrs. Plornish's[1] colloquial style with the delicate accuracy of a sun-picture[2], while there is the same startling inspiration in his description of the gestures and phrases of "Boots,"[3] as in the speeches of Shakespeare's mobs or numskulls, he scarcely ever passes from the humorous and external to the emotional and tragic, without becoming as transcendent in his unreality as he was a moment before in his artistic truthfulness. But for the precious salt of his humour, which compels him to reproduce external traits that serve, in some degree, as a corrective to his

---

1 A character in Charles Dickens' novel *Little Dorrit*.
2 A picture made by means of sunlight, a photograph.
3 Boots (*pl. in form but used as sing.*), the servant in hotels that cleans the boots.

frequently false psychology, his preternaturally virtuous poor children and artisans, his melodramatic boatmen and courtesans, would be as noxious as Eugène Sue's[1] idealized *proletaires* in encouraging the miserable fallacy that high morality and refined sentiment can grow out of harsh social relations, ignorance, and want; or that the working-classes are in a condition to enter at once into a millennial state of *altruism*, wherein everyone is caring for everyone else, and no one for himself.

If we need a true conception of the popular character to guide our sympathies rightly, we need it equally to check our theories, and direct us in their application.[2] The tendency created by the splendid conquests of modern generalization, to believe that all social questions are merged in economical science, and that the relations of men to their neighbours may be settled by algebraic equations, — the dream that the uncultured classes are prepared for a condition which appeals principally to their moral sensibilities, — the aristocratic dilettantism which attempts to restore the "good old times" by a sort of idyllic masquerading, and to grow feudal fidelity and veneration as we grow prize turnips, by an artificial system of culture, — none of these diverging mistakes can co-exist with a real knowledge of the People, with a thorough study of their habits, their ideas, their motives. The landholder, the clergyman, the mill-owner, the mining-agent, have each an opportunity for making precious observations on different sections of the working-classes, but unfortunately their experience is too often not registered at all, or its results are too scattered to be available as a source of information and stimulus to the public mind generally. If any man of sufficient moral

---

1 Eugène Sue (1804–1857), French author of sensational novels dealing with the seamy side of urban life and a leading exponent of the *roman-feuilleton* ("newspaper serial"). His works, often criticized for being melodramatic, were the first to deal with many of the problems that attended the Industrial Revolution in France.
2 In the following ten lines, George Eliot discusses mistakes made by social reformers in trying to "transfer" the peasants to a modern society.

and intellectual breadth, whose observations would not be vitiated by a foregone conclusion, or by a professional point of view, would devote himself to studying the natural history of our social classes, especially of the small shopkeepers, artisans, and peasantry, — the degree in which they are influenced by local conditions, their maxims and habits, the points of view from which they regard their religious teachers, and the degree in which they are influenced by religious doctrines, the interaction of the various classes on each other, and what are the tendencies in their position towards disintegration or towards development, — and if, after all this study, he would give us the result of his observations in a book well nourished with specific facts, his work would be a valuable aid to the social and political reformer ...

The German novelists who undertake to give pictures of peasant-life, fall into the same mistake as our English novelists; they transfer their own feelings to ploughmen and woodcutters, and give them both joys and sorrows of which they know nothing. The peasant never questions the obligation of family-ties — he questions no custom, — but tender affection, as it exists amongst the refined part of mankind, is almost as foreign to him as white hands and filbert-shaped nails. That the aged father who has given up his property to his children on condition of their maintaining him for the remainder of his life, is very far from meeting with delicate attentions, is indicated by the proverb current among the peasantry — "Don't take your clothes off before you go to bed." Among rustic moral tales and parables, not one is more universal than the story of the ungrateful children, who made their grey-headed father, dependent on them for a maintenance, eat at a wooden trough, because he shook the food out of his trembling hands. Then these same ungrateful children observed one day that their own little boy was making a tiny wooden trough; and when they asked him what it was for, he answered — that his father and mother might eat out of it, when he was a man and had to keep them ...

We pay for greater emotional susceptibility too often by nervous diseases of which the peasant knows nothing. To him headache is the least of physical evils, because he thinks headwork the easiest and least indispensable of all labour. Happily, many of the younger sons in peasant families, by going to seek their living in the towns, carry their hardy nervous system to amalgamate with the over-wrought nerves of our town population, and refresh them with a little rude vigour. And a return to the habits of peasant life is the best remedy for many moral as well as physical diseases induced by perverted civilization ... [1]

But many disintegrating forces have been at work on the peasant character, and degeneration is unhappily going on at a greater pace than development. In the wine districts especially, the inability of the small proprietors to bear up under the vicissitudes of the market, or to ensure a high quality of wine by running the risks of a late vintage, and the competition of beer and cider with the inferior wines, have tended to produce that uncertainty of gain which, with the peasant, is the inevitable cause of demoralization. The small peasant proprietors are not a new class in Germany, but many of the evils of their position are new. They are more dependent on ready money than formerly; thus, where a peasant used to get his wood for building and firing from the common forest, he has now to pay for it with hard cash; he used to thatch his own house, with the help perhaps of a neighbour, but now he pays a man to do it for him; he used to pay taxes in kind, he now pays them in money. The chances of the market have to be discounted, and the peasant falls into the hands of money-lenders. Here is one of the cases in which social policy clashes with a purely economical[2] policy.

---

1 In the remainder of the paragraph, George Eliot points out that the native wit of the German peasant, of no avail to him in his painful transfer to modern society, appears to be a powerful assistance in his life on the other side of the Atlantic Ocean.
2 Economic. In contemporary English, "economical" means using money, time and other resources sparingly and carefully.

Political vicissitudes have added their influence to that of economical changes in disturbing that dim instinct, that reverence for traditional custom, which is the peasant's principle of action. He is in the midst of novelties for which he knows no reason — changes in political geography, changes of the government to which he owes fealty, changes in bureaucratic management and police regulations. He finds himself in a new element[1] before an apparatus for breathing in it is developed in him. His only knowledge of modern history is in some of its results — for instance, that he has to pay heavier taxes from year to year. His chief idea of a government is of a power that raises his taxes, opposes his harmless customs, and torments him with new formalities. The source of all this is the false system of "enlightening" the peasant which has been adopted by the bureaucratic governments. A system which disregards the traditions and hereditary attachments of the peasant, and appeals only to a logical understanding which is not yet developed in him, is simply disintegrating and ruinous to the peasant character. The interference with the communal regulations has been of this fatal character. Instead of endeavouring to promote to the utmost the healthy life of the Commune, as an organism the conditions of which are bound up with the historical characteristics of the peasant, the bureaucratic plan of government is bent on improvement by its patent machinery of state-appointed functionaries and off-hand regulations in accordance with modern enlightenment ... Instead of allowing the peasants to manage their own affairs, and, if they happen to believe that five and four make eleven, to unlearn the prejudice by their own experience in calculation, so that they may gradually understand processes, and not merely see results, bureaucracy comes with its "Ready Reckoner" and works all the peasant's sums for him — the surest way of maintaining him in his stupidity, however it

---

1 Any of the four substances — air, water, fire, and earth — formerly believed to compose the physical universe. It may also refer to the state or sphere natural or suited to a person or thing, as water is to fish.

may shake his prejudice ...

Bearing in mind the general characteristics of the German peasant, it is easy to understand his relation to the revolutionary ideas and revolutionary movements of modern times. The peasant, in Germany as elsewhere, is a born grumbler. He has always plenty of grievances in his pocket, but he does not generalize those grievances; he does not complain of "government" or "society," probably because he has good reason to complain of the burgomaster. When a few sparks from the first French Revolution fell among the German peasantry, and in certain villages of Saxony the country people assembled together to write down their demands, there was no glimpse in their petition of the "universal rights of man," but simply of their own particular affairs as Saxon peasants. Again, after the July revolution of 1830, there were many insignificant peasant insurrections; but the object of almost all was the removal of local grievances. Toll-houses were pulled down; stamped paper was destroyed; in some places there was a persecution of wild boars, in others, of that plentiful tame animal, the German *Rath*[1], or councillor who is never called into council. But in 1848, it seemed as if the movements of the peasants had taken a new character; in the small western states of Germany, it seemed as if the whole class of peasantry was in insurrection. But in fact, the peasant did not know the meaning of the part he was playing. He had heard that everything was being set right in the towns, and that wonderful things were happening there, so he tied up his bundle and set off. Without any distinct object or resolution, the country people presented themselves on the scene of commotion, and were warmly received by the party leaders. But, seen from the windows of ducal palaces and ministerial hotels, these swarms of peasants had quite another aspect, and it was imagined that they had a common plan of co-operation. This, however, the peasants have never had. Systematic co-operation implies general conceptions, and a provisional

---

1 In German, "th" is pronounced [t].

subordination of egoism, to which even the artisans of towns have rarely shown themselves equal, and which are as foreign to the mind of the peasant as logarithms or the doctrine of chemical proportions. And the revolutionary fervour of the peasant was soon cooled. The old mistrust of the towns was reawakened on the spot. The Tyrolese peasants saw no great good in the freedom of the press and the constitution because these changes "seemed to please the gentry so much." Peasants who had given their voices stormily for a German parliament, asked afterwards, with a doubtful look, whether it were to consist of infantry or cavalry. When royal domains were declared the property of the State, the peasants in some small principalities rejoiced over this, because they interpreted it to mean that every one would have his share in them, after the manner of the old common and forest rights.

The very practical views of the peasants, with regard to the demands of the people, were in amusing contrast with the abstract theorizing of the educated townsmen. The peasant continually withheld all State payments until he saw how matters would turn out, and was disposed to reckon up the solid benefit, in the form of land or money, that might come to him from the changes obtained. While the townsman was beating his brains about representation on the broadest basis, the peasant asked if the relation between tenant and landlord would continue as before, and whether the removal of the "feudal obligations" meant that the farmer should become owner of the land?

It is in the same naïve way that Communism is interpreted by the German peasantry. The wide spread among them of communistic doctrines, the eagerness with which they listened to a plan for the partition of property, seemed to countenance the notion, that it was a delusion to suppose the peasant would be secured from this intoxication by his love of secure possession and peaceful earnings. But, in fact, the peasant contemplated "partition" by the light of an historical reminiscence rather than of novel theory. The golden age, in the imagination of the peasant, was the time when every member of the commune had a right to as much wood from the forest as would enable him to sell some, after using what he wanted in firing, — in which the communal possessions were so profitable that, instead of his having to pay rates at the end of the year, each member of the commune was something in pocket. Hence the peasants in general understood by "partition," that the State lands, especially the forests, would be divided among the communes, and that, by some political legerdemain or other, everybody would have free fire-wood, free grazing for his cattle, and over and above that, a piece of gold without working for it. That he should give up a single clod of his own to further the general "partition," had never entered the mind of the peasant communist; and the perception that this was an essential preliminary to "partition," was often a sufficient cure for his Communism ...

A significant hint as to the interpretation the peasants put on revolutionary theories, may be drawn from the way they employed the few weeks in which their movements were unchecked. They felled the forest trees and shot the game; they withheld taxes; they shook off the imaginary or real burdens imposed on them by their mediatized princes,[1] by presenting their "demands" in a very rough way before the ducal or princely "Schloss;" they set their faces against the bureaucratic management of the communes, deposed the government functionaries who had been placed over them as burgomasters and magistrates, and abolished the whole bureaucratic system of procedure, simply by taking no notice of its regulations, and recurring to some tradition — some old order or disorder of things. In all this it is clear that they were animated not in the least by the spirit of modern revolution, but by a purely narrow and personal impulse towards reaction.

---

1 To mediatize: (in Germany under the Holy Roman Empire) To reduce (a prince or state) from the position of an immediate vassal of the Empire to that of a mediate vassal. Hence, in later times: To annex (a principality) to another state, leaving to its former sovereign his titular dignity, and (usually) more or less of his rights of government.

The idea of constitutional government lies quite beyond the range of the German peasant's conceptions. His only notion of representation is that of a representation of ranks — of classes; his only notion of a deputy is of one who takes care, not of the national welfare, but of the interests of his own order. Herein lay the great mistake of the democratic party, in common with the bureaucratic governments, that they entirely omitted the peculiar character of the peasant from their political calculations. They talked of the "people," and forgot that the peasants were included in the term. Only a baseless misconception of the peasant's character could induce the supposition that he would feel the slightest enthusiasm about the principles involved in the re-constitution of the Empire, or even about that re-constitution itself. He has no zeal for a written law, as such, but only so far as it takes the form of a living law — a tradition. It was the external authority which the revolutionary party had won in Baden that attracted the peasants into a participation in the struggle.

Such, Riehl[1] tells us, are the general characteristics of the German peasantry — characteristics which subsist amidst a wide variety of circumstances. In Mecklenburg, Pomerania, and Brandenburg, the peasant lives on extensive estates; in Westphalia he lives in large isolated homesteads; in the Westerwald and in Sauerland, in little groups of villages and hamlets; on the Rhine, land is for the most part parcelled out among small proprietors, who live together in large villages. Then, of course, the diversified physical geography of Germany gives rise to equally diversified methods of land-culture; and out of these various circumstances grow numerous specific differences in manner and character. But the generic character of the German peasant is everywhere the same: in the clean mountain hamlet and in the dirty fishing village on

---

1 Wilhelm Heinrich Riehl (1823–1897), German journalist and historian, an influential figure in the rise of sociological history as a discipline. His best-known work is *The Natural History of the German People as a Foundation of German Social Politics*.

the coast; in the plains of North Germany and in the backwoods of America. "Everywhere he has the same historical character — everywhere custom is his supreme law. Where religion and patriotism are still a naïve instinct — are still a sacred custom, there begins the class of the German Peasantry."

...

I. Supplementary information

1. George Eliot

Pseudonym of Mary Ann or Marian Evans, 1819–1880. One of the great English novelists, she was reared in a strict atmosphere of evangelical Protestantism but eventually rebelled and renounced organized religion totally. Her early schooling was supplemented by assiduous reading, and the study of languages led to her first literary work, *The Life of Jesus, Critically Examined* (1846), a translation from the German of D. F. Strauss. After her father's death she became subeditor (1851) of *The Westminster Review*, contributed articles, and came to know many of the literary people of the day. In 1854 she began a long and happy union with G. H. Lewes, which she regarded as marriage, though it involved social ostracism and could have no legal sanction because Lewes's estranged wife was living. Throughout his life Lewes encouraged Evans in her literary career; indeed, it is possible that without him Evans, subject to periods of depression and in constant need of reassurance, would not have written a word.

In 1856, Mary Ann began *Scenes of Clerical Life*, a series of realistic sketches first appearing in *Blackwood's Magazine* under the pseudonym Lewes chose for her, George Eliot. Although not a popular success, the work was well received by literary critics, particularly Dickens and Thackeray. Three novels of provincial life followed — *Adam Bede* (1859), *The Mill on the Floss* (1860), and *Silas Marner* (1861). She visited Italy in 1860 and again in 1861 before she brought out in *The Cornhill Magazine* (1862–1863) her historical romance *Romola*, a story of Savonarola. *Felix Holt* (1866), a political novel, was followed by *The Spanish Gypsy* (1868), a dramatic poem. *Middlemarch* (1871–1872), a portrait of life in a provincial town, is considered her masterpiece. She wrote one more novel, *Daniel Deronda* (1876); the satirical *Impressions of Theophrastus Such* (1879); and verse, which was never popular and is now seldom read. Lewes died in 1878, and in 1880 she married a close friend of both Lewes and herself, John W. Cross, who later edited *George Eliot's Life: as Related in Her Letters and Journals* (3 vol., 1885–1886). Writing about life in small rural towns, George Eliot was primarily concerned with the responsibility that people assume for their lives and with the moral choices they must inevitably make. Although highly serious, her novels are marked by compassion and a subtle humor. (Columbia Encyclopedia)

2. Germany

Germany did not exist as an independent country until late 19th century. The name Germany has long described not a particular place but the loose, fluid polity of Germanic-speaking peoples that held sway over much of western Europe north of the Alps for millennia. Although Germany in that sense is an ancient entity, the German nation in more or less its present form came into being only in the 19th century, when Prussian Prime Minister Otto von Bismarck brought together dozens of German-speaking kingdoms, principalities, free cities, bishoprics, and duchies to form the German Empire in 1871.

The "empire" in our text refers to the Holy Roman Empire, a varying complex of lands in western and central Europe ruled over first by Frankish and then by German kings for ten centuries, from Charlemagne's coronation in 800 until the renunciation of the imperial title in 1806. (Britannica)

3. The Victorian Period

The period in British history coinciding with the reign of Queen Victoria (1837–1901) is commonly divided into three sub-periods.

1) 1832–1851: The Early Victorian Period

This was a time of struggle and growth; the age of the Chartist Movement and the Anti-Corn Law League, but also of the building of railways. "The hungry forties" ended with the Great Exhibition in 1851, the culmination of the Industrial Revolution, which Britain achieved earlier than any other nation.

2) 1851–1870: The Mid-Victorian Period

Britain had passed the time of the worst popular discontents, and was at her height in wealth, power, and influence.

3) 1870–1901: The Late Victorian Period

A less fortunate period, when other nations (especially Germany and the United States) were competing with Britain industrially. Britain had acquired much territory in consequence of her pursuit of trade; she now became imperialist in her jealousy and mistrust of other imperialist nations, and the period ended with the imperialist South African War (Boer War) of 1899–1901. Economically, Britain was becoming less "the workshop of the world" than the world's banker. Domestically, partly in consequence of the second Parliamentary Reform Bill (enfranchising the town workers, 1867) and the Education Act (establishing a state system of education, 1870) it was a time of popular political and social movements which included the building up of trade unions and the formation of the Labour Party.

Culturally, the Victorian period was the age when change rather than stability came first to be accepted as normal in the nature of human outlook.

Ancient foundations of religious belief were eroded, among intellectuals, by scientific advances, especially the biological discoveries of Darwin (Agnosticism). The educated classes and their leaders sought to establish guiding values for living; it was the period of "the Victorian Sage" — Carlyle, Mill, Arnold, Ruskin, and Tennyson — educating the social conscience. The relationship of the individual to himself, to other individuals, and to society at large is the study to which the novel is admirably adapted; the English novel developed in the works of Gaskell, Thackeray, Trollope, the Brontës, Dickens, George Eliot and Henry James into the art form of the age. Culturally and in many ways socially, the Victorian period saw the outset and display of the problems which the 20th century has had to solve. (Prentice Hall Guide)

II. Questions to think about as you read the text

1. What, according to George Eliot, explains the prevalence of rather fictitious and distorted images of peasants in Nineteenth-Century Europe?
2. Why is such representation morally and politically dangerous?
3. What is the most important factor in the peasant's perception of and attitude towards revolution?
4. What according to the author is the greatest obstacle to the peasant's passage into the modern world?

III. Suggested essay topics

1. Sympathizing with ** class (any group of people not initially familiar to you) in the George Eliot style.
2. A case of misrepresentation, of a class, people of a region, a nation or some other group, and the reason(s) underlying such misrepresentation.

IV. Further reading

A Realism of Love[1]

"THIS Rector of Broxton is little better than a pagan!" I hear one of my readers exclaim.

"How much more edifying it would have been if you had made him give Arthur some truly spiritual advice! You might have put into his mouth the most beautiful things — quite as good as reading a sermon."

Certainly I could, if I held it the highest vocation of the novelist to represent things as they never have been and never will be. Then, of course, I might refashion life and character entirely after my own liking; I might select the most unexceptionable type of clergyman and put my own admirable opinions into his mouth on all occasions. But it happens, on the contrary, that my strongest effort is to avoid any such arbitrary picture, and to give a faithful account of men and things as they have mirrored themselves in my mind. The mirror is doubtless defective, the outlines will sometimes be disturbed, the reflection faint or confused; but I feel as much bound to tell you as precisely as I can what that reflection is, as if I were in the witness-box, narrating my experience on oath.

Sixty years ago — it is a long time, so no wonder things have changed — all clergymen were not zealous; indeed, there is reason to believe that the number of zealous clergymen was small, and it is probable that if one among the small minority had owned the livings of Broxton and Hayslope in the year 1799, you would have liked him no better than you like Mr. Irwine. Ten to one, you would have thought him a tasteless, indiscreet, methodistical man. It is so very rarely that facts hit that nice medium required by our own enlightened opinions and refined taste! Perhaps you will say, "Do improve the facts a little, then; make them more accordant

---

[1] From Chapter XVII of *Adam Bede*, a novel by George Eliot.

with those correct views which it is our privilege to possess. The world is not just what we like; do touch it up with a tasteful pencil, and make believe it is not quite such a mixed entangled affair. Let all people who hold unexceptionable opinions act unexceptionably. Let your most faulty characters always be on the wrong side, and your virtuous ones on the right. Then we shall see at a glance whom we are to condemn and whom we are to approve. Then we shall be able to admire, without the slightest disturbance of our prepossessions: we shall hate and despise with that true ruminant relish which belongs to undoubting confidence."

But, my good friend, what will you do then with your fellow-parishioner who opposes your husband in the vestry? With your newly appointed vicar, whose style of preaching you find painfully below that of his regretted predecessor? With the honest servant who worries your soul with her one failing? With your neighbour, Mrs. Green, who was really kind to you in your last illness, but has said several ill-natured things about you since your convalescence? Nay, with your excellent husband himself, who has other irritating habits besides that of not wiping his shoes? These fellow-mortals, every one, must be accepted as they are: you can neither straighten their noses, nor brighten their wit, nor rectify their dispositions; and it is these people — amongst whom your life is passed — that it is needful you should tolerate, pity, and love: it is these more or less ugly, stupid, inconsistent people whose movements of goodness you should be able to admire — for whom you should cherish all possible hopes, all possible patience. And I would not, even if I had the choice, be the clever novelist who could create a world so much better than this, in which we get up in the morning to do our daily work, that you would be likely to turn a harder, colder eye on the dusty streets and the common green fields — on the real breathing men and women, who can be chilled by your indifference or injured by your prejudice; who can be cheered and helped onward by your fellow-feeling, your forbearance, your outspoken, brave justice.

So I am content to tell my simple story, without trying to make things seem better than they were; dreading nothing, indeed, but falsity, which, in spite of one's best efforts, there is reason to dread. Falsehood is so easy, truth so difficult. The pencil is conscious of a delightful facility in drawing a griffin — the longer the claws, and the larger the wings, the better; but that marvellous facility which we mistook for genius is apt to forsake us when we want to draw a real unexaggerated lion. Examine your words well, and you will find that even when you have no motive to be false, it is a very hard thing to say the exact truth, even about your own immediate feelings — much harder than to say something fine about them which is NOT the exact truth.

It is for this rare, precious quality of truthfulness that I delight in many Dutch paintings, which lofty-minded people despise. I find a source of delicious sympathy in these faithful pictures of a monotonous homely existence, which has been the fate of so many more among my fellow-mortals than a life of pomp or of absolute indigence, of tragic suffering or of world-stirring actions. I turn, without shrinking, from cloud-borne angels, from prophets, sibyls, and heroic warriors, to an old woman bending over her flower-pot, or eating her solitary dinner, while the noonday light, softened perhaps by a screen of leaves, falls on her mob-cap, and just touches the rim of her spinning-wheel, and her stone jug, and all those cheap common things which are the precious necessaries of life to her — or I turn to that village wedding, kept between four brown walls, where an awkward bridegroom opens the dance with a high-shouldered, broad-faced bride, while elderly and middle-aged friends look on, with very irregular noses and lips, and probably with quart-pots in their hands, but with an expression of unmistakable contentment and goodwill. "Foh!" says my idealistic friend, "what vulgar details! What good is there in taking all these pains to give an exact likeness of old women and clowns? What a low phase of life! What clumsy, ugly people!"

But bless us, things may be lovable that are not altogether handsome, I hope? I am not at all sure that the majority of the human race have not been ugly, and even among those "lords of their kind," the British, squat figures, ill-shapen nostrils, and dingy complexions are not startling exceptions. Yet there is a great deal of family love amongst us. I have a friend or two whose class of features is such that the Apollo curl on the summit of their brows would be decidedly trying; yet to my certain knowledge tender hearts have beaten for them, and their miniatures — flattering, but still not lovely — are kissed in secret by motherly lips. I have seen many an excellent matron, who could have never in her best days have been handsome, and yet she had a packet of yellow love-letters in a private drawer, and sweet children showered kisses on her sallow cheeks. And I believe there have been plenty of young heroes, of middle stature and feeble beards, who have felt quite sure they could never love anything more insignificant than a Diana, and yet have found themselves in middle life happily settled with a wife who waddles. Yes! Thank God; human feeling is like the mighty rivers that bless the earth: it does not wait for beauty — it flows with resistless force and brings beauty with it.

All honour and reverence to the divine beauty of form! Let us cultivate it to the utmost in men, women, and children — in our gardens and in our houses. But let us love that other beauty too, which lies in no secret of proportion, but in the secret of deep human sympathy. Paint us an angel, if you can, with a floating violet robe, and a face paled by the celestial light; paint us yet oftener a Madonna, turning her mild face upward and opening her arms to welcome the divine glory; but do not impose on us any aesthetic rules which shall banish from the region of Art those old women scraping carrots with their work-worn hands, those heavy clowns taking holiday in a dingy pot-house, those rounded backs and stupid weather-beaten faces that have bent over the spade and done the rough work of the world — those homes with their tin pans, their brown pitchers, their rough curs, and their clusters of onions. In this world there are so many of these common coarse people, who have no picturesque sentimental wretchedness! It is so needful we should remember their existence, else we may happen to leave them quite out of our religion and philosophy and frame lofty theories which only fit a world of extremes. Therefore, let Art always remind us of them; therefore let us always have men ready to give the loving pains of a life to the faithful representing of commonplace things — men who see beauty in these commonplace things, and delight in showing how kindly the light of heaven falls on them. There are few prophets in the world; few sublimely beautiful women; few heroes. I can't afford to give all my love and reverence to such rarities: I want a great deal of those feelings for my every-day fellow-men, especially for the few in the foreground of the great multitude, whose faces I know, whose hands I touch, for whom I have to make way with kindly courtesy. Neither are picturesque lazzaroni or romantic criminals half so frequent as your common labourer, who gets his own bread and eats it vulgarly but creditably with his own pocket-knife. It is more needful that I should have a fibre of sympathy connecting me with that vulgar citizen who weighs out my sugar in a vilely assorted cravat and waistcoat, than with the handsomest rascal in red scarf and green feathers — more needful that my heart should swell with loving admiration at some trait of gentle goodness in the faulty people who sit at the same hearth with me, or in the clergyman of my own parish, who is perhaps rather too corpulent and in other respects is not an Oberlin or a Tillotson, than at the deeds of heroes whom I shall never know except by hearsay, or at the sublimest abstract of all clerical graces that was ever conceived by an able novelist.

The Soul of Man under Socialism[1]

Socialism, Communism, or whatever one chooses to call it, by converting private property into public wealth, and substituting co-operation for competition, will restore society to its proper condition of a thoroughly healthy organism, and insure the material well-being of each member of the community. It will, in fact, give Life its proper basis and its proper environment. But for the full development of Life to its highest mode of perfection, something more is needed. What is needed is Individualism. If the Socialism is Authoritarian; if there are Governments armed with economic power as they are now with political power; if, in a word, we are to have Industrial Tyrannies, then the last state of man will be worse than the first. At present, in consequence of the existence of private property, a great many people are enabled to develop a certain very limited amount of Individualism. They are either under no necessity to work for their living, or are enabled to choose the sphere of activity that is really congenial to them, and gives them pleasure. These are the poets, the philosophers, the men of science, the men of culture — in a word, the real men, the men who have realised themselves, and in whom all Humanity gains a partial realisation. Upon the other hand,

---

[1] By Oscar Wilde, 1891.

there are a great many people who, having no private property of their own, and being always on the brink of sheer starvation, are compelled to do the work of beasts of burden, to do work that is quite uncongenial to them, and to which they are forced by the peremptory, unreasonable, degrading Tyranny of want. These are the poor, and amongst them there is no grace of manner, or charm of speech, or civilisation, or culture, or refinement in pleasures, or joy of life. From their collective force Humanity gains much in material prosperity. But it is only the material result that it gains, and the man who is poor is in himself absolutely of no importance. He is merely the infinitesimal atom of a force that, so far from regarding him, crushes him: indeed, prefers him crushed, as in that case he is far more obedient.

Of course, it might be said that the Individualism generated under conditions of private property is not always, or even as a rule, of a fine or wonderful type, and that the poor, if they have not culture and charm, have still many virtues. Both these statements would be quite true. The possession of private property is very often extremely demoralising, and that is, of course, one of the reasons why Socialism wants to get rid of the institution. In fact, property is really a nuisance. Some years ago people went about the country saying that property has duties. They said it so often and so tediously that, at last, the Church has begun to say it. One hears it now from every pulpit. It is perfectly true. Property not merely has duties, but has so many duties that its possession to any large extent is a bore. It involves endless claims upon one, endless attention to business, endless bother. If property had simply pleasures, we could stand it; but its duties make it unbearable. In the interest of the rich we must get rid of it. The virtues of the poor may be readily admitted, and are much to be regretted. We are often told that the poor are grateful for charity. Some of them are, no doubt, but the best amongst the poor are never grateful. They are ungrateful, discontented, disobedient, and rebellious. They are quite right to be so. Charity they feel to be a ridiculously inadequate mode of partial restitution, or a sentimental dole, usually accompanied by some impertinent attempt on the part of the sentimentalist to tyrannise over their private lives. Why should they be grateful for the crumbs that fall from the rich man's table? They should be seated at the board, and are beginning to know it. As for being discontented, a man who would not be discontented with such surroundings and such a low mode of life would be a perfect brute. Disobedience, in the eyes of anyone who has read history, is man's original virtue. It is through disobedience that progress has been made, through disobedience and through rebellion. Sometimes the poor are praised for being thrifty. But to recommend thrift to the poor is both grotesque and insulting. It is like advising a man who is starving to eat less. For a town or country labourer to practise thrift would be absolutely immoral. Man should not be ready to show that he can live like a badly-fed animal. He should decline to live like that, and should either steal or go on the rates,[1] which is considered by many to be a form of stealing. As for begging, it is safer to beg than to take, but it is finer to take than to beg. No: a poor man who is ungrateful, unthrifty, discontented, and rebellious, is probably a real personality, and has much in him. He is at any rate a healthy protest. As for the virtuous poor, one can pity them, of course, but one cannot possibly admire them. They have made private terms with the enemy, and sold their birthright for very bad pottage. They must also be extraordinarily stupid. I can quite understand a man accepting laws that protect private property, and admit of its accumulation, as long as he himself is able under those conditions to realise some form of beautiful and intellectual life. But it is almost incredible to me how a man whose life is marred and made hideous by such laws can possibly acquiesce in their continuance.

However, the explanation is not really difficult to find. It is simply

---

[1] The phrase "to go on the rates" typically refers to a situation where an individual or a household is receiving financial assistance or support from the government or a public agency. In many countries, such assistance is commonly known as "welfare" or "social assistance."

this. Misery and poverty are so absolutely degrading, and exercise such a paralysing effect over the nature of men, that no class is ever really conscious of its own suffering. They have to be told of it by other people, and they often entirely disbelieve them. What is said by great employers of labour against agitators is unquestionably true. Agitators are a set of interfering, meddling people, who come down to some perfectly contented class of the community, and sow the seeds of discontent amongst them. That is the reason why agitators are so absolutely necessary. Without them, in our incomplete state, there would be no advance towards civilisation. Slavery was put down in America, not in consequence of any action on the part of the slaves, or even any express desire on their part that they should be free. It was put down entirely through the grossly illegal conduct of certain agitators in Boston and elsewhere, who were not slaves themselves, nor owners of slaves, nor had anything to do with the question really. It was, undoubtedly, the Abolitionists who set the torch alight, who began the whole thing. And it is curious to note that from the slaves themselves they received, not merely very little assistance, but hardly any sympathy even; and when at the close of the war the slaves found themselves free, found themselves indeed so absolutely free that they were free to starve, many of them bitterly regretted the new state of things. To the thinker, the most tragic fact in the whole of the French Revolution is not that Marie Antoinette was killed for being a queen, but that the starved peasant of the Vendée[1] voluntarily went out to die for the hideous cause of feudalism.

It is clear, then, that no Authoritarian Socialism will do. For while under the present system a very large number of people can lead lives of a certain

---

1 Vendée is a region in Western France bordering on the Bay of Biscay. During the insurrection of 1793 to 1796, the peasants of the Vendée, who had lived amiably with the local nobility, began violently to oppose the French Revolution when it turned against the Roman Catholic Church. Under Henri La Rochejaquelein and others, an army of more than 50,000 men was raised to clear the region of Revolutionary authorities.

amount of freedom and expression and happiness, under an industrial-barrack system, or a system of economic tyranny, nobody would be able to have any such freedom at all. It is to be regretted that a portion of our community should be practically in slavery, but to propose to solve the problem by enslaving the entire community is childish. Every man must be left quite free to choose his own work. No form of compulsion must be exercised over him. If there is, his work will not be good for him, will not be good in itself, and will not be good for others. And by work I simply mean activity of any kind.

I hardly think that any Socialist, nowadays, would seriously propose that an inspector should call every morning at each house to see that each citizen rose up and did manual labour for eight hours. Humanity has got beyond that stage, and reserves such a form of life for the people whom, in a very arbitrary manner, it chooses to call criminals. But I confess that many of the socialistic views that I have come across seem to me to be tainted with ideas of authority, if not of actual compulsion. Of course, authority and compulsion are out of the question. All association must be quite voluntary. It is only in voluntary associations that man is fine.

But it may be asked how Individualism, which is now more or less dependent on the existence of private property for its development, will benefit by the abolition of such private property. The answer is very simple. It is true that, under existing conditions, a few men who have had private means of their own, such as Byron, Shelley, Browning, Victor Hugo, Baudelaire, and others, have been able to realise their personality more or less completely. Not one of these men ever did a single day's work for hire. They were relieved from poverty. They had an immense advantage. The question is whether it would be for the good of Individualism that such an advantage should be taken away. Let us suppose that it is taken away. What happens then to Individualism? How will it benefit?

It will benefit in this way. Under the new conditions Individualism will be far freer, far finer, and far more intensified than it is now. I am not talking of the great imaginatively-realised Individualism of such poets as I have mentioned, but of the great actual Individualism latent and potential in mankind generally. For the recognition of private property has really harmed Individualism, and obscured it, by confusing a man with what he possesses. It has led Individualism entirely astray. It has made gain not growth its aim. So that man thought that the important thing was to have, and did not know that the important thing is to be. The true perfection of man lies, not in what man has, but in what man is.

Private property has crushed true Individualism, and set up an Individualism that is false. It has debarred one part of the community from being individual by starving them. It has debarred the other part of the community from being individual by putting them on the wrong road, and encumbering them. Indeed, so completely has man's personality been absorbed by his possessions that the English law has always treated offences against a man's property with far more severity than offences against his person, and property is still the test of complete citizenship. The industry necessary for the making money is also very demoralising. In a community like ours, where property confers immense distinction, social position, honour, respect, titles, and other pleasant things of the kind, man, being naturally ambitious, makes it his aim to accumulate this property, and goes on wearily and tediously accumulating it long after he has got far more than he wants, or can use, or enjoy, or perhaps even know of. Man will kill himself by overwork in order to secure property, and really, considering the enormous advantages that property brings, one is hardly surprised. One's regret is that society should be constructed on such a basis that man has been forced into a groove in which he cannot freely develop what is wonderful, and fascinating, and delightful in him — in which, in fact, he misses the true pleasure and joy of living. He is also, under existing conditions, very insecure. An enormously wealthy merchant may be — often is — at every moment of his life at the mercy of things that are not under his control. If the wind blows an extra point or so, or the weather suddenly changes, or some trivial thing happens, his ship may go down, his speculations may go wrong, and he finds himself a poor man, with his social position quite gone. Now, nothing should be able to harm a man except himself. Nothing should be able to rob a man at all. What a man really has, is what is in him. What is outside of him should be a matter of no importance.

With the abolition of private property, then, we shall have true, beautiful, healthy Individualism. Nobody will waste his life in accumulating things, and the symbols for things. One will live. To live is the rarest thing in the world. Most people exist, that is all.

I. Supplementary information

1. Oscar Wilde

Oscar Wilde, born on October 16, 1854, in Dublin, Ireland, into an intellectual and artistic family, was a renowned Irish playwright, novelist, poet, and wit, who became one of the most prominent figures in the late 19th-century literary scene.

Wilde's education was distinguished, and he studied at Trinity College, Dublin and later at Magdalen College, Oxford, where he excelled in classics and cultivated his love for literature. Known for his wit, flamboyant personality, and sharp tongue, Wilde quickly gained recognition as a charismatic figure in social and literary circles.

In the 1880s, Wilde established himself as a playwright, writing several successful comedies that blended satire, wit, and social commentary. His most famous works include *The Importance of Being Earnest, An Ideal*

Husband, and *Lady Windermere's Fan*. These plays showcased Wilde's trademark epigrammatic style and clever dialogue, earning him widespread acclaim.

Beyond his accomplishments in theater, Wilde was also a prolific writer of essays, short stories, and poetry. His only novel, *The Picture of Dorian Gray*, published in 1890, is considered a classic of English literature and explores themes of art, decadence, and the duality of human nature.

However, Wilde's life took a tragic turn when his homosexuality, considered a criminal offense at the time, was exposed. In 1895, he was convicted of "gross indecency" and sentenced to two years of hard labor. The experience took a toll on Wilde's health and reputation, and he lived in exile in France after his release.

Despite his personal hardships, Wilde left an indelible mark on literature and aesthetics. His works continue to be celebrated for their wit, social commentary, and exploration of human nature.

2. The Aesthetic Movement

Aestheticism, also referred to as the Aesthetic Movement, was an influential art movement that emerged in the late 19th century, primarily in Europe and the United States. Known by its creed of "art for art's sake," the movement emphasized the pursuit of beauty, elegance, and sensory pleasure in all aspects of life.

Rejecting the dominant Victorian ideals of moral and social responsibility, Aestheticism sought to challenge traditional norms and promote individual freedom of expression, and celebrated the aesthetic experience as a valuable end in itself.

Aestheticism encompassed various art forms, including literature, visual arts, design, and interior decoration. Prominent figures associated with the movement include Oscar Wilde, Walter Pater, James McNeill Whistler, and Aubrey Beardsley, among others. These individuals championed the idea that art should not be bound by moral or didactic purposes but should instead exist purely to provide pleasure and stimulate the senses.

Aestheticism challenged the conventional boundaries between art and life, advocating for the integration of beauty into everyday existence. It influenced various fields, including fashion, interior design, and even lifestyle choices, as adherents sought to create harmonious and aesthetically pleasing environments.

II. Questions to think about as you read the text

1. Where does the harm of private property lie according to Oscar Wilde? Would Virginia Woolf, author of "A Room of One's Own," agree with him on this issue?
2. Which parts of this excerpt show Wilde's rejection of mainstream Victorian values?

III. Suggested essay topics

1. Write an essay comparing views of John Stuart Mill and Oscar Wilde expressed in the two excerpts included in this textbook.
2. Write an essay in response to Wilde's creed of "art for art's sake." You may base your discussion on specific works of art with which you are familiar.

IV. Further reading

Preface to *The Picture of Dorian Gray*

    THE artist is the creator of beautiful things.

    To reveal art and conceal the artist is art's aim.

    The critic is he who can translate into another manner or a new material his impression of beautiful things.

The highest as the lowest form of criticism is a mode of autobiography.

Those who find ugly meanings in beautiful things are corrupt without being charming. This is a fault.

Those who find beautiful meanings in beautiful things are the cultivated. For these there is hope.

They are the elect to whom beautiful things mean only Beauty.

There is no such thing as a moral or an immoral book.

Books are well written, or badly written. That is all.

The nineteenth century dislike of Realism is the rage of Caliban seeing his own face in a glass.

The nineteenth century dislike of Romanticism is the rage of Caliban not seeing his own face in a glass.

The moral life of man forms part of the subject-matter of the artist, but the morality of art consists in the perfect use of an imperfect medium.

No artist desires to prove anything. Even things that are true can be proved.

No artist has ethical sympathies. An ethical sympathy in an artist is an unpardonable mannerism of style.

No artist is ever morbid. The artist can express everything.

Thought and language are to the artist instruments of an art.

Vice and virtue are to the artist materials for an art.

From the point of view of form, the type of all the arts is the art of the musician. From the point of view of feeling, the actor's craft is the type.

All art is at once surface and symbol.

Those who go beneath the surface do so at their peril.

Those who read the symbol do so at their peril.

It is the spectator, and not life, that art really mirrors.

Diversity of opinion about a work of art shows that the work is new, complex, and vital.

When critics disagree the artist is in accord with himself.

We can forgive a man for making a useful thing as long as he does not admire it. The only excuse for making a useless thing is that one admires it intensely.

All art is quite useless.

Oscar Wilde

Letter from a Birmingham Jail[1]

My Dear Fellow Clergymen:

While confined here in the Birmingham city jail, I came across your recent statement calling my present activities "unwise and untimely." Seldom do I pause to answer criticism of my work and ideas. If I sought to answer all the criticisms that cross my desk, my secretaries would have little time for anything other than such correspondence in the course of the day, and I would have no time for constructive work. But since I feel that you are men of genuine good will and that your criticisms are sincerely set forth, I want to try to answer your statement in what I hope will be patient and reasonable terms.

I think I should indicate why I am here in Birmingham, since you

---

[1] By Martin Luther King, Jr., written on April 16, 1963, while King was jailed for civil disobedience; subsequently published in *Why We Can't Wait* (1964). Author's note: This response to a published statement by eight fellow clergymen from Alabama was composed under somewhat constricting circumstance. Begun on the margins of the newspaper in which the statement appeared while I was in jail, the letter was continued on scraps of writing paper supplied by a friendly Negro trusty, and concluded on a pad my attorneys were eventually permitted to leave me. Although the text remains in substance unaltered, I have indulged in the author's prerogative of polishing it for publication.

have been influenced by the view which argues against "outsiders coming in." I have the honor of serving as president of the Southern Christian Leadership Conference, an organization operating in every southern state, with headquarters in Atlanta, Georgia. We have some eighty-five affiliated organizations across the South, and one of them is the Alabama Christian Movement for Human Rights. Frequently we share staff, educational and financial resources with our affiliates. Several months ago the affiliate here in Birmingham asked us to be on call to engage in a nonviolent direct action program if such were deemed necessary. We readily consented, and when the hour came we lived up to our promise. So I, along with several members of my staff, am here because I was invited here. I am here because I have organizational ties here.

But more basically, I am in Birmingham because injustice is here. Just as the prophets of the eighth century B.C. left their villages and carried their "thus saith the Lord" far beyond the boundaries of their home towns, and just as the Apostle Paul left his village of Tarsus and carried the gospel of Jesus Christ to the far corners of the Greco-Roman world, so am I compelled to carry the gospel of freedom beyond my own home town. Like Paul, I must constantly respond to the Macedonian call for aid.

Moreover, I am cognizant of the interrelatedness of all communities and states. I cannot sit idly by in Atlanta and not be concerned about what happens in Birmingham. Injustice anywhere is a threat to justice everywhere. We are caught in an inescapable network of mutuality, tied in a single garment of destiny. Whatever affects one directly, affects all indirectly. Never again can we afford to live with the narrow, provincial "outside agitator" idea. Anyone who lives inside the United States can never be considered an outsider anywhere within its bounds.

You deplore the demonstrations taking place in Birmingham. But your statement, I am sorry to say, fails to express a similar concern for the conditions that brought about the demonstrations. I am sure that none of you would want to rest content with the superficial kind of social analysis that deals merely with effects and does not grapple with underlying causes. It is unfortunate that demonstrations are taking place in Birmingham, but it is even more unfortunate that the city's white power structure left the Negro community with no alternative.

In any nonviolent campaign there are four basic steps: collection of the facts to determine whether injustices exist; negotiation; self-purification; and direct action. We have gone through all these steps in Birmingham. There can be no gainsaying the fact that racial injustice engulfs this community. Birmingham is probably the most thoroughly segregated city in the United States. Its ugly record of brutality is widely known. Negroes have experienced grossly unjust treatment in the courts. There have been more unsolved bombings of Negro homes and churches in Birmingham than in any other city in the nation. These are the hard, brutal facts of the case. On the basis of these conditions, Negro leaders sought to negotiate with the city fathers. But the latter consistently refused to engage in good-faith negotiation.

Then, last September, came the opportunity to talk with leaders of Birmingham's economic community. In the course of the negotiations, certain promises were made by the merchants — for example, to remove the stores' humiliating racial signs. On the basis of these promises, the Reverend Fred Shuttlesworth and the leaders of the Alabama Christian Movement for Human Rights agreed to a moratorium on all demonstrations. As the weeks and months went by, we realized that we were the victims of a broken promise. A few signs, briefly removed, returned; the others remained. As in so many past experiences, our hopes had been blasted, and the shadow of deep disappointment settled upon us. We had no alternative except to prepare for direct action, whereby we would present our very bodies as a means of laying our case before the conscience of the local and the national community. Mindful of the difficulties involved, we decided to undertake a process of self-purification. We began a series of workshops on nonviolence, and we repeatedly asked ourselves: "Are you able to accept blows without retaliating?" "Are you able to endure the ordeal of jail?" We decided to schedule our direct action program for the Easter season, realizing that except for Christmas, this is the main shopping period of the year. Knowing that a strong economic-withdrawal program would be the by-product of direct action, we felt that this would be the best time to bring pressure to bear on the merchants for the needed change.

Then it occurred to us that Birmingham's mayoral election was coming up in March, and we speedily decided to postpone action until after election day. When we discovered that the Commissioner of Public Safety, Eugene "Bull" Connor, had piled up enough votes to be in the run-off, we decided again to postpone action until the day after the run-off so that the demonstrations could not be used to cloud the issues. Like many others, we waited to see Mr. Connor defeated, and to this end we endured postponement after postponement. Having aided in this community need, we felt that our direct action program could be delayed no longer.

You may well ask: "Why direct action? Why sit-ins, marches and so forth? Isn't negotiation a better path?" You are quite right in calling for negotiation. Indeed, this is the very purpose of direct action. Nonviolent direct action seeks to create such a crisis and foster such a tension that a community which has constantly refused to negotiate is forced to confront the issue. It seeks so to dramatize the issue that it can no longer be ignored. My citing the creation of tension as part of the work of the nonviolent resister may sound rather shocking. But I must confess that I am not afraid of the word "tension." I have earnestly opposed violent tension, but there is a type of constructive, nonviolent tension which is necessary for growth. Just as Socrates felt that it was necessary to create a tension in the mind so that individuals could rise from the bondage of myths and half-truths to the unfettered realm of creative analysis and objective appraisal, so must we see the need for nonviolent gadflies to create the kind of tension in society that will help men rise from the dark depths of prejudice and racism to the majestic heights of understanding and brotherhood. The purpose of our direct-action program is to create a situation so crisis-packed that it will inevitably open the door to negotiation. I therefore concur with you in your call for negotiation. Too long has our beloved Southland been bogged down in a tragic effort to live in monologue rather than dialogue.

One of the basic points in your statement is that the action that I and my associates have taken in Birmingham is untimely. Some have asked: "Why didn't you give the new city administration time to act?" The only answer that I can give to this query is that the new Birmingham administration must be prodded about as much as the outgoing one, before it will act. We are sadly mistaken if we feel that the election of Albert Boutwell as mayor will bring the millennium to Birmingham. While Mr. Boutwell is a much more gentle person than Mr. Connor, they are both segregationists, dedicated to maintenance of the status quo. I have hope that Mr. Boutwell will be reasonable enough to see the futility of massive resistance to desegregation. But he will not see this without pressure from devotees of civil rights. My friends, I must say to you that we have not made a single gain in civil rights without determined legal and nonviolent pressure. Lamentably, it is an historical fact that privileged groups seldom give up their privileges voluntarily. Individuals may see the moral light and voluntarily give up their unjust posture; but, as Reinhold Niebuhr has reminded us, groups tend to be more immoral than individuals.

We know through painful experience that freedom is never voluntarily given by the oppressor; it must be demanded by the oppressed. Frankly, I have yet to engage in a direct-action campaign that was "well timed" in the view of those who have not suffered unduly from the disease of segregation. For years now I have heard the word "Wait!" It rings in the ear of every Negro with piercing familiarity. This "Wait" has almost always meant "Never." We must come to see, with one of our distinguished jurists, that "justice too long delayed is justice denied."

We have waited for more than 340 years for our constitutional and God-given rights. The nations of Asia and Africa are moving with jetlike speed toward gaining political independence, but we still creep at horse-and-buggy pace toward gaining a cup of coffee at a lunch counter. Perhaps it is easy for those who have never felt the stinging darts of segregation to say, "Wait." But when you have seen vicious mobs lynch your mothers and fathers at will and drown your sisters and brothers at whim; when you have seen hate-filled policemen curse, kick and even kill your black brothers and sisters; when you see the vast majority of your twenty million Negro brothers smothering in an airtight cage of poverty in the midst of an affluent society; when you suddenly find your tongue twisted and your speech stammering as you seek to explain to your six-year-old daughter why she can't go to the public amusement park that has just been advertised on television, and see tears welling up in her eyes when she is told that Funtown is closed to colored children, and see ominous clouds of inferiority beginning to form in her little mental sky, and see her beginning to distort her personality by developing an unconscious bitterness toward white people; when you have to concoct an answer for a five-year-old son who is asking: "Daddy, why do white people treat colored people so mean?"; when you take a cross-county drive and find it necessary to sleep night after night in the uncomfortable corners of your automobile because no motel will accept you; when you are humiliated day in and day out by nagging signs reading "white" and "colored"; when your first name becomes "nigger," your middle name becomes "boy" (however old you are) and your last name becomes "John," and your wife and mother are never given the respected title "Mrs."; when you are harried by day and haunted by night by the fact that you are a Negro, living constantly at tiptoe stance, never quite knowing what to expect next, and are plagued with inner fears and outer resentments; when you are forever fighting a degenerating sense of "nobodiness" — then you will understand why we find it difficult to wait. There comes a time when the cup of endurance runs over, and men are no longer willing to be plunged into the abyss of despair. I hope, sirs, you can understand our legitimate and unavoidable impatience. You express a great deal of anxiety over our willingness to break laws. This is certainly a legitimate concern. Since we so diligently urge people to obey the Supreme Court's decision of 1954 outlawing segregation in the public schools, at first glance it may seem rather paradoxical for us consciously to break laws. One may well ask: "How can you advocate breaking some laws and obeying others?" The answer lies in the fact that there are two types of laws: just and unjust. I would be the first to advocate obeying just laws. One has not only a legal but a moral responsibility to obey just laws. Conversely, one has a moral responsibility to disobey unjust laws. I would agree with St. Augustine that "an unjust law is no law at all."

Now, what is the difference between the two? How does one determine whether a law is just or unjust? A just law is a man-made code that squares with the moral law or the law of God. An unjust law is a code that is out of harmony with the moral law. To put it in the terms of St. Thomas Aquinas: An unjust law is a human law that is not rooted in eternal law and natural law. Any law that uplifts human personality is just. Any law that degrades human personality is unjust. All segregation statutes are unjust because segregation distorts the soul and damages the personality. It gives the segregator a false sense of superiority and the segregated a false sense of inferiority. Segregation, to use the terminology of the Jewish philosopher Martin Buber, substitutes an "I it" relationship for an "I thou" relationship and ends up relegating persons to the status of things. Hence segregation is not only politically, economically and sociologically unsound, it is morally wrong and sinful. Paul Tillich has said that sin is separation. Is not segregation an existential expression of man's tragic separation, his awful estrangement, his terrible sinfulness? Thus it is that I can urge men to obey the 1954 decision of the Supreme Court, for it is morally right; and I can urge them to disobey segregation ordinances, for they are morally wrong.

Let us consider a more concrete example of just and unjust laws. An unjust law is a code that a numerical or power majority group compels a minority group to obey but does not make binding on itself. This is difference made legal. By the same token, a just law is a code that a majority compels a minority to follow and that it is willing to follow itself. This is sameness made legal. Let me give another explanation. A law is unjust if it is inflicted on a minority that, as a result of being denied the right to vote, had no part in enacting or devising the law. Who can say that the legislature of Alabama which set up that state's segregation laws was democratically elected? Throughout Alabama all sorts of devious methods are used to prevent Negroes from becoming registered voters, and there are some counties in which, even though Negroes constitute a majority of the population, not a single Negro is registered. Can any law enacted under such circumstances be considered democratically structured?

Sometimes a law is just on its face and unjust in its application. For instance, I have been arrested on a charge of parading without a permit. Now, there is nothing wrong in having an ordinance which requires a permit for a parade. But such an ordinance becomes unjust when it is used to maintain segregation and to deny citizens the First-Amendment privilege of peaceful assembly and protest.

I hope you are able to see the distinction I am trying to point out. In no sense do I advocate evading or defying the law, as would the rabid segregationist. That would lead to anarchy. One who breaks an unjust law must do so openly, lovingly, and with a willingness to accept the penalty. I submit that an individual who breaks a law that conscience tells him is unjust, and who willingly accepts the penalty of imprisonment in order to arouse the conscience of the community over its injustice, is in reality expressing the highest respect for law.

Of course, there is nothing new about this kind of civil disobedience. It was evidenced sublimely in the refusal of Shadrach, Meshach and Abednego to obey the laws of Nebuchadnezzar[1], on the ground that a higher moral law was at stake. It was practiced superbly by the early Christians, who were willing to face hungry lions and the excruciating pain of chopping blocks rather than submit to certain unjust laws of the Roman Empire. To a degree, academic freedom is a reality today because Socrates practiced civil disobedience.[2] In our own nation, the Boston Tea Party represented a massive act of civil disobedience.

We should never forget that everything Adolf Hitler did in Germany was "legal" and everything the Hungarian freedom fighters[3] did in Hungary was "illegal." It was "illegal" to aid and comfort a Jew in Hitler's Germany. Even so, I am sure that, had I lived in Germany at the time, I would have aided and comforted my Jewish brothers. If today I lived in a Communist country where certain principles dear to the Christian faith are suppressed, I would openly advocate disobeying that country's anti-religious laws.

I must make two honest confessions to you, my Christian and Jewish brothers. First, I must confess that over the past few years I have been gravely disappointed with the white moderate. I have almost reached the regrettable conclusion that the Negro's great stumbling block in his stride toward freedom is not the White Citizen's Counciler or the Ku Klux Klanner, but the white moderate, who is more devoted to "order" than to justice; who prefers a negative peace which is the absence of tension to a positive peace which is the presence of justice; who constantly says: "I agree with you in the goal you seek, but I cannot agree with your methods of direct action;"

---

1 The story is told in Daniel 3.
2 The ancient Greek philosopher Socrates was tried by the Athenians for corrupting their youth through his sceptical, questioning manner of teaching. He refused to change his ways and was condemned to death.
3 In the anti-Communist revolution of 1956, which was quickly put down by the Soviet army.

who paternalistically believes he can set the timetable for another man's freedom; who lives by a mythical concept of time and who constantly advises the Negro to wait for a "more convenient season." Shallow understanding from people of good will is more frustrating than absolute misunderstanding from people of ill will. Lukewarm acceptance is much more bewildering than outright rejection.

I had hoped that the white moderate would understand that law and order exist for the purpose of establishing justice and that when they fail in this purpose, they become the dangerously structured dams that block the flow of social progress. I had hoped that the white moderate would understand that the present tension in the South is a necessary phase of the transition from an obnoxious negative peace, in which the Negro passively accepted his unjust plight, to a substantive and positive peace, in which all men will respect the dignity and worth of human personality. Actually, we who engage in nonviolent direct action are not the creators of tension. We merely bring to the surface the hidden tension that is already alive. We bring it out in the open, where it can be seen and dealt with. Like a boil that can never be cured so long as it is covered up but must be opened with all its ugliness to the natural medicines of air and light, injustice must be exposed, with all the tension its exposure creates, to the light of human conscience and the air of national opinion before it can be cured.

In your statement you assert that our actions, even though peaceful, must be condemned because they precipitate violence. But is this a logical assertion? Isn't this like condemning a robbed man because his possession of money precipitated the evil act of robbery? Isn't this like condemning Socrates because his unswerving commitment to truth and his philosophical inquiries precipitated the act by the misguided populace in which they made him drink hemlock? Isn't this like condemning Jesus because his unique God consciousness and never-ceasing devotion to God's will precipitated the evil act of crucifixion? We must come to see that, as the federal courts have consistently affirmed, it is wrong to urge an individual to cease his efforts to gain his basic constitutional rights because the quest may precipitate violence. Society must protect the robbed and punish the robber. I had also hoped that the white moderate would reject the myth concerning time in relation to the struggle for freedom. I have just received a letter from a white brother in Texas. He writes: "All Christians know that the colored people will receive equal rights eventually, but it is possible that you are in too great a religious hurry. It has taken Christianity almost two thousand years to accomplish what it has. The teachings of Christ take time to come to earth." Such an attitude stems from a tragic misconception of time, from the strangely irrational notion that there is something in the very flow of time that will inevitably cure all ills. Actually, time itself is neutral; it can be used either destructively or constructively. More and more I feel that the people of ill will have used time much more effectively than have the people of good will. We will have to repent in this generation not merely for the hateful words and actions of the bad people but for the appalling silence of the good people. Human progress never rolls in on wheels of inevitability; it comes through the tireless efforts of men willing to be co-workers with God, and without this hard work, time itself becomes an ally of the forces of social stagnation. We must use time creatively, in the knowledge that the time is always ripe to do right. Now is the time to make real the promise of democracy and transform our pending national elegy into a creative psalm of brotherhood. Now is the time to lift our national policy from the quicksand of racial injustice to the solid rock of human dignity.

You speak of our activity in Birmingham as extreme. At first I was rather disappointed that fellow clergymen would see my nonviolent efforts as those of an extremist. I began thinking about the fact that I stand in the middle of two opposing forces in the Negro community. One is a force of complacency, made up in part of Negroes who, as a result of long years of oppression, are so drained of self-respect and a sense of "somebodiness" that they have adjusted to segregation; and in part of a few middle-class Negroes who, because of a degree of academic and economic security and because in some ways they profit by segregation, have become insensitive to the problems of the masses. The other force is one of bitterness and hatred, and it comes perilously close to advocating violence. It is expressed in the various black nationalist groups that are springing up across the nation, the largest and best known being Elijah Muhammad's Muslim movement.[1] Nourished by the Negro's frustration over the continued existence of racial discrimination, this movement is made up of people who have lost faith in America, who have absolutely repudiated Christianity, and who have concluded that the white man is an incorrigible "devil."

I have tried to stand between these two forces, saying that we need emulate neither the "do nothingism" of the complacent nor the hatred and despair of the black nationalist. For there is the more excellent way of love and nonviolent protest. I am grateful to God that, through the influence of the Negro church, the way of nonviolence became an integral part of our struggle.

If this philosophy had not emerged, by now many streets of the South would, I am convinced, be flowing with blood. And I am further convinced that if our white brothers dismiss as "rabble rousers" and "outside agitators" those of us who employ nonviolent direct action, and if they refuse to support our nonviolent efforts, millions of Negroes will, out of frustration and despair, seek solace and security in black nationalist ideologies — a development that would inevitably lead to a frightening racial nightmare.

Oppressed people cannot remain oppressed forever. The yearning for freedom eventually manifests itself, and that is what has happened to the American Negro. Something within has reminded him of his birthright of

---

1 Elijah Muhammad (1897–1975) succeeded to the leadership of the "Nation of Islam" in 1934.

freedom, and something without has reminded him that it can be gained. Consciously or unconsciously, he has been caught up by the *Zeitgeist*[1], and with his black brothers of Africa and his brown and yellow brothers of Asia, South America and the Caribbean, the United States Negro is moving with a sense of great urgency toward the promised land of racial justice. If one recognizes this vital urge that has engulfed the Negro community, one should readily understand why public demonstrations are taking place. The Negro has many pent-up resentments and latent frustrations, and he must release them. So let him march; let him make prayer pilgrimages to the city hall; let him go on freedom rides and try to understand why he must do so. If his repressed emotions are not released in nonviolent ways, they will seek expression through violence; this is not a threat but a fact of history. So I have not said to my people: "Get rid of your discontent." Rather, I have tried to say that this normal and healthy discontent can be channelled into the creative outlet of nonviolent direct action. And now this approach is being termed extremist.

But though I was initially disappointed at being categorized as an extremist, as I continued to think about the matter, I gradually gained a measure of satisfaction from the label. Was not Jesus an extremist for love: "Love your enemies, bless them that curse you, do good to them that hate you, and pray for them which despitefully use you, and persecute you." Was not Amos an extremist for justice: "Let justice roll down like waters and righteousness like an ever-flowing stream." Was not Paul an extremist for the Christian gospel: "I bear in my body the marks of the Lord Jesus." Was not Martin Luther an extremist: "Here I stand; I cannot do otherwise, so help me God." And John Bunyan[2]: "I will stay in jail to the end of my days

---

1 The spirit of the times.
2 Amos was an Old Testament prophet; Paul, a New Testament apostle; Luther (1483–1546), German Protestant reformer; Bunyan, English preacher and author (1628–1688).

before I make a butchery of my conscience." And Abraham Lincoln: "This nation cannot survive half slave and half free." And Thomas Jefferson: "We hold these truths to be self-evident, that all men are created equal ..." So the question is not whether we will be extremists, but what kind of extremists we will be. Will we be extremists for hate or for love? Will we be extremists for the preservation of injustice or for the extension of justice? In that dramatic scene on Calvary's hill three men were crucified. We must never forget that all three were crucified for the same crime — the crime of extremism. Two were extremists for immorality, and thus fell below their environment. The other, Jesus Christ, was an extremist for love, truth and goodness, and thereby rose above his environment. Perhaps the South, the nation and the world are in dire need of creative extremists.

I had hoped that the white moderate would see this need. Perhaps I was too optimistic; perhaps I expected too much. I suppose I should have realized that few members of the oppressor race can understand the deep groans and passionate yearnings of the oppressed race, and still fewer have the vision to see that injustice must be rooted out by strong, persistent and determined action. I am thankful, however, that some of our white brothers in the South have grasped the meaning of this social revolution and committed themselves to it. They are still all too few in quantity, but they are big in quality. Some — such as Ralph McGill, Lillian Smith, Harry Golden, James McBride Dabbs, Ann Braden and Sarah Patton Boyle — have written about our struggle in eloquent and prophetic terms. Others have marched with us down nameless streets of the South. They have languished in filthy, roach-infested jails, suffering the abuse and brutality of policemen who view them as "dirty nigger-lovers." Unlike so many of their moderate brothers and sisters, they have recognized the urgency of the moment and sensed the need for powerful "action" — antidotes to combat the disease of segregation.

Let me take note of my other major disappointment. I have been so greatly disappointed with the white church and its leadership. Of course, there are some notable exceptions. I am not unmindful of the fact that each of you has taken some significant stands on this issue. I commend you, Reverend Stallings, for your Christian stand on this past Sunday, in welcoming Negroes to your worship service on a nonsegregated basis. I commend the Catholic leaders of this state for integrating Spring Hill College several years ago.

But despite these notable exceptions, I must honestly reiterate that I have been disappointed with the church. I do not say this as one of those negative critics who can always find something wrong with the church. I say this as a minister of the gospel, who loves the church; who was nurtured in its bosom; who has been sustained by its spiritual blessings and who will remain true to it as long as the cord of life shall lengthen.

When I was suddenly catapulted into the leadership of the bus protest in Montgomery, Alabama, a few years ago,[1] I felt we would be supported by the white church. I felt that the white ministers, priests and rabbis of the South would be among our strongest allies. Instead, some have been outright opponents, refusing to understand the freedom movement and misrepresenting its leaders; all too many others have been more cautious than courageous and have remained silent behind the anesthetizing security of stained-glass windows.

In spite of my shattered dreams, I came to Birmingham with the hope that the white religious leadership of this community would see the justice of our cause and, with deep moral concern, would serve as the channel through which our just grievances could reach the power structure. I had hoped that each of you would understand. But again I have been disappointed.

I have heard numerous southern religious leaders admonish their worshipers to comply with a desegregation decision because it is the law, but I have longed to hear white ministers declare: "Follow this decree because integration is morally right and because the Negro is your brother."

---

1 In December 1955, when Rosa Parks refused to move to the back of a bus.

In the midst of blatant injustices inflicted upon the Negro, I have watched white churchmen stand on the sideline and mouth pious irrelevancies and sanctimonious trivialities. In the midst of a mighty struggle to rid our nation of racial and economic injustice, I have heard many ministers say: "Those are social issues, with which the gospel has no real concern." And I have watched many churches commit themselves to a completely other-worldly religion which makes a strange, un-Biblical distinction between body and soul, between the sacred and the secular.

I have traveled the length and breadth of Alabama, Mississippi and all the other southern states. On sweltering summer days and crisp autumn mornings I have looked at the South's beautiful churches with their lofty spires pointing heavenward. I have beheld the impressive outlines of her massive religious education buildings. Over and over I have found myself asking: "What kind of people worship here? Who is their God? Where were their voices when the lips of Governor Barnett dripped with words of interposition and nullification? Where were they when Governor Wallace gave a clarion call for defiance and hatred?[1] Where were their voices of support when bruised and weary Negro men and women decided to rise from the dark dungeons of complacency to the bright hills of creative protest?"

Yes, these questions are still in my mind. In deep disappointment I have wept over the laxity of the church. But be assured that my tears have been tears of love. There can be no deep disappointment where there is not deep love. Yes, I love the church. How could I do otherwise? I am in the rather unique position of being the son, the grandson and the great grandson of preachers. Yes, I see the church as the body of Christ. But, oh! How we have blemished and scarred that body through social neglect and through fear of

---

1 Ross Barnett (1898–1988), governor of Mississippi, opposed James Meredith's admission to the University of Mississippi; George Wallace (1919–1998), governor of Alabama, opposed admission of several black students to the University of Alabama.

being nonconformists.

There was a time when the church was very powerful — in the time when the early Christians rejoiced at being deemed worthy to suffer for what they believed. In those days the church was not merely a thermometer that recorded the ideas and principles of popular opinion; it was a thermostat that transformed the mores of society. Whenever the early Christians entered a town, the people in power became disturbed and immediately sought to convict the Christians for being "disturbers of the peace" and "outside agitators." But the Christians pressed on, in the conviction that they were "a colony of heaven," called to obey God rather than man. Small in number, they were big in commitment. They were too God-intoxicated to be "astronomically intimidated." By their effort and example they brought an end to such ancient evils as infanticide and gladiatorial contests.

Things are different now. So often the contemporary church is a weak, ineffectual voice with an uncertain sound. So often it is an arch-defender of the status quo. Far from being disturbed by the presence of the church, the power structure of the average community is consoled by the church's silent — and often even vocal — sanction of things as they are.

But the judgment of God is upon the church as never before. If today's church does not recapture the sacrificial spirit of the early church, it will lose its authenticity, forfeit the loyalty of millions, and be dismissed as an irrelevant social club with no meaning for the twentieth century. Every day I meet young people whose disappointment with the church has turned into outright disgust.

Perhaps I have once again been too optimistic. Is organized religion too inextricably bound to the status quo to save our nation and the world? Perhaps I must turn my faith to the inner spiritual church, the church within the church, as the true ekklesia[1] and the hope of the world. But again I am

---

1 The Greek New Testament word for the early Christian church.

thankful to God that some noble souls from the ranks of organized religion have broken loose from the paralyzing chains of conformity and joined us as active partners in the struggle for freedom. They have left their secure congregations and walked the streets of Albany, Georgia, with us. They have gone down the highways of the South on tortuous rides for freedom. Yes, they have gone to jail with us. Some have been dismissed from their churches, have lost the support of their bishops and fellow ministers. But they have acted in the faith that right defeated is stronger than evil triumphant. Their witness has been the spiritual salt that has preserved the true meaning of the gospel in these troubled times. They have carved a tunnel of hope through the dark mountain of disappointment.

I hope the church as a whole will meet the challenge of this decisive hour. But even if the church does not come to the aid of justice, I have no despair about the future. I have no fear about the outcome of our struggle in Birmingham, even if our motives are at present misunderstood. We will reach the goal of freedom in Birmingham and all over the nation, because the goal of America is freedom. Abused and scorned though we may be, our destiny is tied up with America's destiny. Before the pilgrims landed at Plymouth, we were here. Before the pen of Jefferson etched the majestic words of the Declaration of Independence across the pages of history, we were here. For more than two centuries our forebears labored in this country without wages; they made cotton king; they built the homes of their masters while suffering gross injustice and shameful humiliation — and yet out of a bottomless vitality they continued to thrive and develop. If the inexpressible cruelties of slavery could not stop us, the opposition we now face will surely fail. We will win our freedom because the sacred heritage of our nation and the eternal will of God are embodied in our echoing demands.

Before closing I feel impelled to mention one other point in your statement that has troubled me profoundly. You warmly commended the Birmingham police force for keeping "order" and "preventing violence." I doubt that you would have so warmly commended the police force if you had seen its dogs sinking their teeth into unarmed, nonviolent Negroes. I doubt that you would so quickly commend the policemen if you were to observe their ugly and inhumane treatment of Negroes here in the city jail; if you were to watch them push and curse old Negro women and young Negro girls; if you were to see them slap and kick old Negro men and young boys; if you were to observe them, as they did on two occasions, refuse to give us food because we wanted to sing our grace together. I cannot join you in your praise of the Birmingham police department.

It is true that the police have exercised a degree of discipline in handling the demonstrators. In this sense they have conducted themselves rather "nonviolently" in public. But for what purpose? To preserve the evil system of segregation. Over the past few years I have consistently preached that nonviolence demands that the means we use must be as pure as the ends we seek. I have tried to make clear that it is wrong to use immoral means to attain moral ends. But now I must affirm that it is just as wrong, or perhaps even more so, to use moral means to preserve immoral ends. Perhaps Mr. Connor and his policemen have been rather nonviolent in public, as was Chief Pritchett in Albany, Georgia, but they have used the moral means of nonviolence to maintain the immoral end of racial injustice. As T. S. Eliot has said: "The last temptation is the greatest treason: To do the right deed for the wrong reason."[1]

I wish you had commended the Negro sit-inners and demonstrators of Birmingham for their sublime courage, their willingness to suffer and their amazing discipline in the midst of great provocation. One day the South will recognize its real heroes. They will be the James Merediths[2], with the noble

---

1   American-born English poet (1888–1965), the lines are from his play *Murder in the Cathedral*.
2   Meredith was the first black to enroll at the University of Mississippi.

sense of purpose that enables them to face jeering and hostile mobs, and with the agonizing loneliness that characterizes the life of the pioneer. They will be old, oppressed, battered Negro women, symbolized in a seventy-two-year-old woman in Montgomery, Alabama, who rose up with a sense of dignity and with her people decided not to ride segregated buses, and who responded with ungrammatical profundity to one who inquired about her weariness: "My feets is tired, but my soul is at rest." They will be the young high school and college students, the young ministers of the gospel and a host of their elders, courageously and nonviolently sitting in at lunch counters and willingly going to jail for conscience' sake. One day the South will know that when these disinherited children of God sat down at lunch counters, they were in reality standing up for what is best in the American dream and for the most sacred values in our Judaeo-Christian heritage, thereby bringing our nation back to those great wells of democracy which were dug deep by the founding fathers in their formulation of the Constitution and the Declaration of Independence.

Never before have I written so long a letter. I'm afraid it is much too long to take your precious time. I can assure you that it would have been much shorter if I had been writing from a comfortable desk, but what else can one do when he is alone in a narrow jail cell, other than write long letters, think long thoughts and pray long prayers?

If I have said anything in this letter that overstates the truth and indicates an unreasonable impatience, I beg you to forgive me. If I have said anything that understates the truth and indicates my having a patience that allows me to settle for anything less than brotherhood, I beg God to forgive me.

I hope this letter finds you strong in the faith. I also hope that circumstances will soon make it possible for me to meet each of you, not as an integrationist or a civil-rights leader but as a fellow clergyman and a Christian brother. Let us all hope that the dark clouds of racial prejudice will soon pass away and the deep fog of misunderstanding will be lifted from our fear-drenched communities, and in some not-too-distant tomorrow the radiant stars of love and brotherhood will shine over our great nation with all their scintillating beauty.

Yours for the cause of Peace and Brotherhood,
King, Martin Luther Jr.

I. Supplementary information

1. The Montgomery bus boycott

The Montgomery bus boycott was a seminal event in the Civil Rights Movement that took place in Montgomery, Alabama, in 1955–1956. It was a collective act of protest against racial segregation on public buses and served as a catalyst for larger efforts to challenge racial inequality in the United States. The boycott was triggered by the arrest of Rosa Parks, an African American woman who refused to give up her seat to a white passenger on a Montgomery city bus. Her act of defiance on December 1, 1955, ignited a wave of outrage and galvanized the African American community. The movement led to a 1956 U.S. Supreme Court decision declaring that Montgomery's segregation laws on buses were unconstitutional. The 381-day bus boycott also brought the Rev. Martin Luther King, Jr., into the spotlight as one of the most important leaders of the American civil rights movement.

2. Ku Klux Klan

The Ku Klux Klan (KKK) is a white supremacist hate group that has existed in the United States since the late 1860s. The organization has gone through multiple incarnations over its history, but its central ideology remains rooted in racism, xenophobia, and the preservation of white supremacy.

The KKK was first established in Pulaski, Tennessee, in 1865, shortly after the American Civil War. Its primary aim was to intimidate and oppress African Americans who had recently gained freedom from slavery. The Klan used violence and terrorism to maintain white dominance and prevent social and political equality for Black Americans.

During its initial formation, the Klan targeted newly freed slaves and their supporters, including white Republicans and African American leaders who advocated for civil rights. The Klan's influence waned during the Reconstruction era, but it experienced a resurgence in the early 20th century, coinciding with the rise of xenophobic and nativist sentiments. During this period, the KKK expanded its targets beyond African Americans and directed its hatred toward immigrants, Catholics, Jews, and other minority groups deemed as threats to their vision of a homogenous white America.

II. Questions to think about as you read the text

1. Pay attention to King's frequent use of metaphors. What effect do they achieve?
2. What is the use of historical figures in this speech?
3. How does King defend the protesters' breaking of laws?

III. Suggested essay questions

1. Racism (or other forms of hatred/discrimination, based on gender, class, region, nationality, etc.) in disguise. Write an essay on how such -ism often takes seemingly non-controversial forms.
2. Identify a specific social or political problem that you would like to see

addressed. Present two contrasting arguments: an immediate solution, or a graduated approach.

IV. Further reading

On August 28, 1963, during the March on Washington for Jobs and Freedom, Martin Luther King Jr. delivered what was to be one of the most iconic and influential speeches in American history.

I Have a Dream

I am happy to join with you today in what will go down in history as the greatest demonstration for freedom in the history of our nation.

Five score years ago, a great American, in whose symbolic shadow we stand today, signed the Emancipation Proclamation. This momentous decree came as a great beacon light of hope to millions of Negro slaves who had been seared in the flames of withering injustice. It came as a joyous daybreak to end the long night of their captivity.

But one hundred years later, the Negro still is not free. One hundred years later, the life of the Negro is still sadly crippled by the manacles of segregation and the chains of discrimination. One hundred years later, the Negro lives on a lonely island of poverty in the midst of a vast ocean of material prosperity. One hundred years later, the Negro is still languished in the corners of American society and finds himself an exile in his own land. And so we've come here today to dramatize a shameful condition.

In a sense we've come to our nation's capital to cash a check. When the architects of our republic wrote the magnificent words of the Constitution and the Declaration of Independence, they were signing a promissory note to which every American was to fall heir. This note was a promise that all men, yes, black men as well as white men, would be guaranteed the "unalienable Rights" of "Life, Liberty and the pursuit of Happiness." It is obvious today that America has defaulted on this promissory note, insofar as her citizens of color are concerned. Instead of honoring this sacred obligation, America has given the Negro people a bad check, a check which has come back marked "insufficient funds."

But we refuse to believe that the bank of justice is bankrupt. We refuse to believe that there are insufficient funds in the great vaults of opportunity of this nation. And so, we've come to cash this check, a check that will give us upon demand the riches of freedom and the security of justice.

We have also come to this hallowed spot to remind America of the fierce urgency of now. This is no time to engage in the luxury of cooling off or to take the tranquilizing drug of gradualism. Now is the time to make real the promises of democracy. Now is the time to rise from the dark and desolate valley of segregation to the sunlit path of racial justice. Now is the time to lift our nation from the quicksands of racial injustice to the solid rock of brotherhood. Now is the time to make justice a reality for all of God's children.

It would be fatal for the nation to overlook the urgency of the moment. This sweltering summer of the Negro's legitimate discontent will not pass until there is an invigorating autumn of freedom and equality. Nineteen sixty-three is not an end, but a beginning. And those who hope that the Negro needed to blow off steam and will now be content will have a rude awakening if the nation returns to business as usual. And there will be neither rest nor tranquility in America until the Negro is granted his citizenship rights. The whirlwinds of revolt will continue to shake the foundations of our nation until the bright day of justice emerges.

But there is something that I must say to my people, who stand on the warm threshold which leads into the palace of justice: In the process of gaining our rightful place, we must not be guilty of wrongful deeds. Let us not seek to satisfy our thirst for freedom by drinking from the cup of bitterness and hatred. We must forever conduct our struggle on the high plane of dignity and discipline. We must not allow our creative protest to degenerate into physical violence. Again and again, we must rise to the majestic heights of meeting physical force with soul force.

The marvelous new militancy which has engulfed the Negro community must not lead us to a distrust of all white people, for many of our white brothers, as evidenced by their presence here today, have come to realize that their destiny is tied up with our destiny. And they have come to realize that their freedom is inextricably bound to our freedom.

We cannot walk alone.

And as we walk, we must make the pledge that we shall always march ahead.

We cannot turn back.

There are those who are asking the devotees of civil rights, "When will you be satisfied?" We can never be satisfied as long as the Negro is the victim of the unspeakable horrors of police brutality. We can never be satisfied as long as our bodies, heavy with the fatigue of travel, cannot gain lodging in the motels of the highways and the hotels of the cities. We cannot be satisfied as long as the negro's basic mobility is from a smaller ghetto to a larger one. We can never be satisfied as long as our children are stripped of their self-hood and robbed of their dignity by signs stating: "For Whites Only." We cannot be satisfied as long as a Negro in Mississippi cannot vote and a Negro in New York believes he has nothing for which to vote. No, no, we are not satisfied, and we will not be satisfied until "justice rolls down like waters, and righteousness like a mighty stream."

I am not unmindful that some of you have come here out of great trials and tribulations. Some of you have come fresh from narrow jail cells. And some of you have come from areas where your quest — quest for freedom left you battered by the storms of persecution and staggered by the winds of police brutality. You have been the veterans of creative suffering. Continue to work with the faith that unearned suffering is redemptive. Go back to Mississippi, go back to Alabama, go back to South Carolina, go back to

Georgia, go back to Louisiana, go back to the slums and ghettos of our northern cities, knowing that somehow this situation can and will be changed.

Let us not wallow in the valley of despair, I say to you today, my friends.

And so even though we face the difficulties of today and tomorrow, I still have a dream. It is a dream deeply rooted in the American dream.

I have a dream that one day this nation will rise up and live out the true meaning of its creed: "We hold these truths to be self-evident, that all men are created equal."

I have a dream that one day on the red hills of Georgia, the sons of former slaves and the sons of former slave owners will be able to sit down together at the table of brotherhood.

I have a dream that one day even the state of Mississippi, a state sweltering with the heat of injustice, sweltering with the heat of oppression, will be transformed into an oasis of freedom and justice.

I have a dream that my four little children will one day live in a nation where they will not be judged by the color of their skin but by the content of their character.

I have a dream today!

I have a dream that one day, down in Alabama, with its vicious racists, with its governor having his lips dripping with the words of "interposition" and "nullification" — one day right there in Alabama little black boys and black girls will be able to join hands with little white boys and white girls as sisters and brothers.

I have a dream today!

I have a dream that one day every valley shall be exalted, and every hill and mountain shall be made low, the rough places will be made plain, and the crooked places will be made straight; "and the glory of the Lord shall be revealed and all flesh shall see it together."

This is our hope, and this is the faith that I go back to the South with.

With this faith, we will be able to hew out of the mountain of despair a stone of hope. With this faith, we will be able to transform the jangling discords of our nation into a beautiful symphony of brotherhood. With this faith, we will be able to work together, to pray together, to struggle together, to go to jail together, to stand up for freedom together, knowing that we will be free one day.

And this will be the day — this will be the day when all of God's children will be able to sing with new meaning:

My country 'tis of thee, sweet land of liberty, of thee I sing. Land where my fathers died, land of the Pilgrim's pride,

From every mountainside, let freedom ring!

And if America is to be a great nation, this must become true.

And so let freedom ring from the prodigious hilltops of New Hampshire.

Let freedom ring from the mighty mountains of New York.

Let freedom ring from the heightening Alleghenies of Pennsylvania.

Let freedom ring from the snow-capped Rockies of Colorado.

Let freedom ring from the curvaceous slopes of California.

But not only that:

Let freedom ring from Stone Mountain of Georgia.

Let freedom ring from Lookout Mountain of Tennessee.

Let freedom ring from every hill and molehill of Mississippi.

From every mountainside, let freedom ring.

And when this happens, and when we allow freedom ring, when we let it ring from every village and every hamlet, from every state and every city, we will be able to speed up that day when all of God's children, black men and white men, Jews and Gentiles, Protestants and Catholics, will be able to join hands and sing in the words of the old Negro spiritual:

Free at last! Free at last!

Thank God Almighty, we are free at last!

Martin Luther King, Jr 1963

图书在版编目(CIP)数据

西方人文思想选篇精读:英文/苏耕欣主编. —上海:复旦大学出版社,2023.12(2025.5 重印)
ISBN 978-7-309-16583-8

Ⅰ.①西… Ⅱ.①苏… Ⅲ.①思想史-西方国家-英文 Ⅳ.①B5

中国版本图书馆 CIP 数据核字(2022)第 204449 号

西方人文思想选篇精读
苏耕欣　主编
责任编辑/方尚芩

复旦大学出版社有限公司出版发行
上海市国权路 579 号　邮编:200433
网址:fupnet@fudanpress.com　http://www.fudanpress.com
门市零售:86-21-65102580　团体订购:86-21-65104505
出版部电话:86-21-65642845
常熟市华顺印刷有限公司

开本 787 毫米×1092 毫米　1/16　印张 13　字数 193 千字
2023 年 12 月第 1 版
2025 年 5 月第 1 版第 4 次印刷

ISBN 978-7-309-16583-8/B·769
定价:56.00 元

如有印装质量问题,请向复旦大学出版社有限公司出版部调换。
版权所有　侵权必究